Bold Amazing Message From God

THIS BOOK BELONGS TO

_____

Volume 1

Copyright © 2024 JJFH International

All rights reserved. No part of this book may be reproduced or utilized in any form or by any means, electronic or mechanical, including photocopying, recording or by any information storage retrieval system, without permission in writing from the publisher.

ISBN 9798352542200

Acknowledgements

I would first like to thank my God, my Lord and Savior Jesus Christ and the Holy Spirit for these Bold Amazing Messages. These messages have taught me and have given me a deeper revelation of who God is and who we are in God.

I would like to thank my amazing and wonderful husband for all of your support and for covering me and loving me in this amazing covenant we have with God.

I would like to thank all of our children, family and friends for your amazing support.

I would like to thank our awesome daughter, Summer Raaine Fox, for editing this book. You have done an amazing job. You are such a powerful young woman.

I would like to thank **The Walking Club** for all of your support. We have all been in class together, receiving God's teachings through these BAMs. Let's continue to walk this thing out Tuesday - Friday at 8:30am EST!

A special thank you to my momma.

When the Lord told you I was His mouthpiece, you believed it until the day you stood before Him.

Forward

JJ and the BAM "The Bold Amazing Message From God" have changed my life and have taught me so much since I started following her Facebook lives on The Walking Club. I knew the moment she called me out by name, that God was speaking to her and through her to me. When JJ says she loves you and there is nothing you can do about it—there is nothing you can do but to accept it, embrace it and know she loves you with all her heart. She speaks truth into my life daily through the BAM and I know without a doubt that I have personally grown from it. Each BAM is a learning experience not only for myself but for everyone who experiences it. Proverbs 27:17 states, "As iron sharpens iron, so a friend sharpens a friend." If you want to be sharpened, if you want a word to penetrate your heart, to transform and renew your mind, heart and soul—this BAM is for you! You will not be the same after reading it and experiencing it. The BAM is the real deal. It is the truth and nothing but the truth. In Jesus name! Glory! Hallelujah. Thank you for your obedience, JJ and know that I love you and there ain't nothing you can do about it!!

Amy G. Bearden

God is here.
There is no doubt about it.
He's given us clarity and relief
When our mind has been crowded
Bold and Amazing
Yes, Bold and Amazing is He.
God, thank you for these messages that have given me so much relief.
Relief from myself
Relief from my flesh
You reached out Your Hand
To call me into Your very best
You have made me new
Made me new with every word
My cup has overflown
With each BAM that I have heard
God, I thank you for the BAMs
I know these Words to be true
I thank you for experiencing a new level in You
I thank you for Your Goodness
And every Word You have deemed Truth
And each Bold Amazing Message
That has given us break through

Summer Raaine Fox

As I watched her, I became so intrigued. This was the perfect love story. I watched how the relationship grew deeper and deeper. I watched how they would spend countless hours, one on one in each other's presence and talking to one another. I watched the happiness and the glow on her face after each conversation. I watched how love overtook her and the way she started loving others with the same type of love. This was a true love, an agape love, a love taught by God himself. A love between HER and her God and out of this love, birthed the Bold Amazing Message from God.

Yes, the HER is JJ Fox Hatch. I watched JJ's growth as she developed her relationship with God and pursued her purpose. The BAM is one of the greatest God given miracles that come from this relationship and here is why I call it a miracle. I watch JJ as she gets up every morning around 3:00 am and goes in the presence of the Lord and comes out with the BAM. There's no studying or manuscripts involved. God wants it to be His Word and His Word alone. This is the BAM that JJ brings to you daily. I've experienced this for over 3 years and I'm still in awe of God's miracle. BAM is an amazing book. I would encourage everyone to get this book. This book is so versatile, and you get a different revelation every time you read it. It can be used in study groups or as an individual study guide.

My Love, I am so proud of you and how you have allowed God to use you. I watch souls being saved everyday while listening to you. You are truly God's mouthpiece, and this is only the beginning. I love you and there's nothing you can do about it.

Your Loving Husband
Darryl S Hatch Sr.

Disclaimer

I am JJ Fox Hatch and I have conversations with God. What does that mean? That means that I speak to God and He speaks to me, that means that I get into His Presence, and I listen to Him.

Believe it or not I have not always had these conversations with God. I had to build my own personal relationship with Him. I had to release all of the unforgiveness that was inside of me and get into His Word for myself. I had to ask Him to help me to remove hatred, bitterness and unforgiveness out of my heart, while building my own faith and trust in Him. I could no longer depend on my mother to talk to God for me or to pray to get me out of situations that I put myself in. I had to pray to Him for myself. I could no longer get by with knowing of Him; I had to really get to know Him. When I got to know Him, everything changed. My life changed, my mind changed, and my heart changed. He's not only my God; He became my Friend.

Every morning, the Lord wakes me up to come into His Presence. While I am in His presence, He speaks. I write down every word He speaks, and these words are the messages He wants His children to know. God calls these messages, The Bold Amazing Messages From God. These messages are given to us by God Himself. In these messages, you can receive a deeper revelation of His Words, while experiencing His Voice.

Now this is the most important part of my disclaimer. I am not the only one that God wants to speak to or speak through. Yes, God speaks through the pastors, teachers, apostles, evangelists and the prophets, but God wants to speak to each and every one of His children, and that includes you. God wants you to know how much He loves you. He wants you to know that He is there for you. Spend some time in His presence and build a deeper relationship with your Lord and Savior Jesus Christ. These Bold Amazing Messages from God are the words from God's Mouth into your ears. Get your own confirmation and keep your mouth off of folks.

I love you and there is nothing that you can do about it… AYYEEE OHHH

JJ Fox Hatch

Bold Amazing Message From God

Table of Contents

I AM GOD 19

Time Of The Manna *(Supernatural Provision)*................................ 23

Breadcrumbs *(Don't See Yourself As Small)* 27

Hear My Voice *(Know The Voice of God)* 31

My Yoke Is Easy, My Burden Is Light *(No Load That We Should Carry)* 35

It's My Bill *(Don't Worry, Don't Try To Figure It Out)* 38

Outweigh The Wait *(Wait on God)* 42

What You See vs What I Say *(God's Word is Truth)* 46

Rollover *(Financial Blessings From Generation to Generation)* 50

My Teachings *(Don't Forget My Teachings)* 54

War of Words *(What You Speak)* 58

Cover The Table *(I Prepared The Table You Will Serve From)* 62

Purpose Not Magic *(God Is Not A Magic Trick)*. 68

Hope In Glory *(You Are No Longer Enthusiastic About God)* 71

Hairline *(The Line to Receive and Not To Receive Is Thin)* 76

Reassemble *(God Will Put Us Back Together)* 80

Raise Your Shield *(Raise Your Shield of Faith)* 84

Hidden Treasures *(You Have Hidden Treasures Inside You)* 88

A Heart of a Carpenter *(Help Build My Kingdom)* 92

Heart - Attacks *(Guard Your Heart)* 95

Fight *(Fight For What God Has For You)* 99

There Is A Shift *(And It Will Be Uncomfortable)* 103

Go! Possess It! *(Take Ownership)* 107

House of Prayer *(Direct Communication To God)* 111

Backsteps Will Never Move You Forward *(Don't Go Back Into Sin)* 115

The Catcher and The Thief *(The Enemy Can Steal Your Words)* 119

The Power of Divine Connections 123

Ready or Not, Here I Come *(Jesus is Coming)* 127

I Am Closing Doors 131

Chasing The Mist *(The Cloud, The Fog, The Haze)* 134

Walking Sturdy *(Consistency With God)* 138

Give Me Permission *(Say Yes To God)* 141

Pinpoint It *(Pinpoint Your Gifts and Talents)* 144

The Ability to Discern *(Ask For Discernment)* 148

The Power Of Rejection *(Has God's Protection)* 152

Don't Be Surprised *(Don't Be Surprised With What You See In This World)* 156

Struggles *(Release All Struggles To God)* 160

Become Skillful *(Preparation In God's Presence)* 164

Pick A Team *(What Team Will You Choose?)* 168

Remembrance *(Remember That God Is There For You)* 172

Boldness *(Boldness in God)* 176

Weeping *(God's Children are Weeping Over The Wrong Things)* 180

Scoffer *(Don't Worry About The Scoffers)* 184

Rely On God *(God Is Your Source)* 188

When You Are Weak, I Am Strong *(Your Strength Comes From God)* 192

It Is In You *(God's Power Is In Us)* 196

Fireplace *(A Fire Within Us)* 200

Rebuild *(Rebuild Your Relationship With God)* 204

Preparation | Warning *(A Storm Is Coming For This World)* 208

Reliable *(Are You Reliable?)* 212

Serve Me First *(I AM First)* 215

My Thoughts *(What God Thinks About You)* 219

Breakthrough *(Spiritual Revival)* 223

Outburst *(Sudden Blessings)* 226

More Valuable Than Money *(The Principles Of God)* 230

Clarity & Direction *(God Is Leading Us)* 235

Define Yourself In Me *(Tell Your Story)* 239

Wrestle *(Fighting Against Peace)* 243

Set Apart (*God Has Set You Apart*) 247

Obedience Is Priceless *(The Cost Of Disobedience is Famine)* 250

Pray *(Time To Pray)* 254

Prayer Of Commitment 258

Decrees 259

The Armor Of God 263

Thankful *(What are you thankful to God for?)* 265

About The Author 270

BAM! BAM! BAM! BAM! BAM!

What is BAM, Ms. JJ? What is BAM?

BAM is that Bold Amazing Message From God

BAM is this fresh manna that we're getting in this book

BAM are the words out of God's mouth into your ears

BAM will be your teaching

BAM will be your leading

BAM will be your guidance

And BAM

is the very thing that you need to go to God and get your own confirmation!

Keep your mouth off of folks!

In Jesus name!

I AM GOD

''Some of My children do not have a clue of who I really am. For if you knew, you would rest. If you knew, you would have the confidence in who I AM. My children, I AM Alpha and Omega, The First and The Last, The Beginning and The End. There is no one before Me or after Me. I AM The Lord your God. In Me, your enemies are defeated, for I have already defeated them. At the name of Jesus, demons tremble, and in My Presence, evil runs. Armies can not stop Me. Nations can not hold Me. Who AM I? Do not delay in finding out who I AM in your life. Do not delay knowing who is on your side, saith the Lord.

My children, I created this Earth and in My Time, I will end the very evil that has held you back. I AM God and there is no other god. I AM your Father. I have given you My Power, My Strength. I AM the God who gave you victory, the God who causes you to be more than conquerors. You are winners in Me; know that you were created for the winning team. My children, if you knew Me, really knew Me, you would not fear the very things you have the power to rebuke. There would be less crying and screaming out My Name and more confidence that it is all in My Hands. My children, why do you not know who I AM? Really know who I AM? Why do you choose not to believe who you are in Me? I AM the Lord your God: your Protector, Provider, your Waymaker. I AM that I AM.

My children, do not live in the not knowing, not knowing who I AM. Not knowing who I AM will not make you safe, but a target for the devil. When you know who I AM, you would not hide; you would not run from your enemy, but stand firm, knowing that I AM your God. I have conquered everything on this Earth and beneath this Earth. My children, that same power is in you. When you know who I AM, you will know who you are. When you know who I AM, you will know who is on your side. My children, I AM the Lord your God, who reigns and rules forever. Nothing and no one can stand against you, for I AM your God, saith the Lord.''

Exodus 3 : 14 (NKJV) - *''And God said to Moses, "I AM WHO I AM." And He said, "Thus you shall say to the children of Israel, 'I AM has sent me to you.'''*

Acts 7 : 32 (ESV) - *'' 'I am the God of your fathers, the God of Abraham and of Isaac and of Jacob.' ''*

Isaiah 44 : 24 (ESV) - *''Thus says the LORD, your Redeemer, who formed you from the womb: 'I am the LORD, who made all things, who alone stretched out the heavens, who spread out the earth by myself,' ''*

Revelation 22 : 13 (ESV) - *'' 'I am the Alpha and the Omega, the first and the last, the beginning and the end.' ''*

NOTES

What revelation did you receive from this BAM?

_____
_____
_____
_____
_____

Do you know who God is? Describe who God is to you.

_____
_____
_____
_____
_____

Name 5 ways you can increase your understanding of who God is.

_____
_____
_____
_____
_____

NOTES

TIME OF THE MANNA
(Supernatural Provision)

''This is the time when My children trust and depend only on Me, saith the Lord. My children, in the time of famine for others, it will be the time of manna for you. When there is famine on the earth, there will be an overflow of My Blessings, My Manna; a supernatural supply. This manna, this supernatural provision will be given to those who trust and obey Me. This is not the time to disobey Me and this is not the time not to trust My Word, saith the Lord; for the time of famine is here, and the time to receive My Manna is now! Trust and depend only on Me and I will provide for you, saith the Lord.''

JJ's VISION: After God spoke, He showed me a vision of His Foot on the enemy's head, and I asked Him why I was seeing this. He told me that "I am preventing the enemy from interfering in the supernatural provision that I have for you. There will be no interference, saith the Lord.''

Manna: The miraculous bread of heaven, God's Supernatural Provision

Supernatural Provision: Divine Provision, God providing for our every need in a way that exceeds natural expectations and understanding

---

Psalm 37 : 25 - 26 (ESV) - *"I have been young, and now am old, yet I have not seen the righteous forsaken or his children begging for bread. He is ever lending generously and his children become a blessing."*

Psalm 34 : 10 (ESV) - *"The young lions suffer want and hunger; but those who seek the LORD lack no good thing."*

Psalm 23 : 1 (ESV) - *"The LORD is my shepherd; I shall not want."*

Philippians 4 : 19 (ESV) - *"And my God will supply every need of yours according to his riches in glory in Christ Jesus."*

NOTES

What revelation did you receive from this BAM?

_____
_____
_____
_____
_____

Do you believe in God's supernatural provision? What does supernatural provision mean to you?

_____
_____
_____
_____
_____

How can you trust and obey God to live in His supernatural provision?

_____
_____
_____
_____
_____

NOTES

BREADCRUMBS

(Don't See Yourself As Small)

''My children, there is no comparison between a loaf of bread and breadcrumbs. What you see as little, I make greater. What you see as bigger, I make it grander. My Thoughts of you have never been small. In every area of your life, you have the room, the capacity to hold what I have given you, saith the Lord.

My children, when the anointing of My Spirit comes upon you, there is nothing that can hold you down or hold you back. You are thinking of yourself as small. You have become comfortable with thinking and saying: 'I am only going to get breadcrumbs.' I am here telling you there is no comparison between the loaf or the crumbs. When My anointing is over you, no longer see yourself as small, when it is I who lives in you. No longer feel that the breadcrumbs are all you will get or have. Know who I AM. I AM the Breadmaker. I AM the Architect of your life. I custom built the very things that are inside of you. You have the capacity to move in My Greatness. My Greatness is in you. Never feel small with a Big God, saith the Lord.

My children, it is time to show you who I AM. Think about it. I AM God. The God that is bigger than you can imagine, but yet, I live in you. The capacity in you can hold more than you know, more than you can understand and take you further than you can go. So, when you say, 'I am only going to get breadcrumbs in my life,' how are you seeing the breadcrumbs? Do you see them only as small? What are you doing with them? Tell Me. How much do you believe that the Greater One lives inside of you? How much do you believe that there is nothing I can not do? There is nothing too small or too big that your Father can not produce to be greater. I turn breadcrumbs into a loaf and a loaf into more loaves and more loaves. Do you believe it? Change your thinking to think bigger. Let's go, saith the Lord."

Luke 9 : 16 (AMP) - *"Then He took the five loaves and the two fish, and He looked up to heaven [and gave thanks] and blessed them, and broke them and kept giving them to the disciples to set before the crowd."*

John 6 : 35 (ESV) - *"Jesus said to them, 'I am the bread of life; whoever comes to me shall not hunger, and whoever believes in me shall never thirst.'"*

2 Corinthians 9 : 10 (ESV) - *"He who supplies seed to the sower and bread for food will supply and multiply your seed for sowing and increase the harvest of your righteousness."*

NOTES

What revelation did you receive from this BAM?

_____
_____
_____
_____
_____

Are there things in your life that make you see yourself as small?

_____
_____
_____
_____
_____

How do you go from thinking small to believing big?

_____
_____
_____
_____
_____

NOTES

HEAR MY VOICE

(Know The Voice of God)

"I want My children to hear My Voice. I want My children to know My Voice. I am speaking to My children, with great urgency, saith the Lord. The time has come when you must know My Voice. My Voice speaks loud through My Words. My Word is My Voice, but My children are struggling to hear My Voice. I want My children to hear My Voice and to know My Voice, saith the Lord. The enemy can deceive you when you don't know My Voice. My sheep know My Voice.

My children, My Voice speaks loud through My Word. My Word is My Voice. My Peace is My Voice. My Love is My Voice. The Holy Spirit carries My Voice. Listen to My Voice. Hear My Voice, saith the Lord."

John 10 : 27 (ESV) - *"My sheep hear my voice, and I know them, and they follow me."*

John 10 : 14 (ESV) - *"I am the good shepherd. I know my own and my own know me,"*

John 10 : 1 - 5 (MSG) - *"Let me set this before you as plainly as I can. If a person climbs over or through the fence of a sheep pen instead of going through the gate, you know he's up to no good—a sheep rustler! The shepherd walks right up to the gate. The gatekeeper opens the gate to him and the sheep recognize his voice. He calls his own sheep by name and leads them out. When he gets them all out, he leads them and they follow because they are familiar with his voice. They won't follow a stranger's voice but will scatter because they aren't used to the sound of it."*

NOTES

What revelation did you receive from this BAM?

_____
_____
_____
_____
_____

Do you know/recognize the Voice of the Lord? Describe a time when you knew God was speaking to you.

_____
_____
_____
_____
_____

How can you know the Voice of the Lord even more?

_____
_____
_____
_____
_____

NOTES

MY YOKE IS EASY, MY BURDEN IS LIGHT
(No Load That We Should Carry)

"Today is a good day to let you know that I AM here. There is no load you should carry, for I AM here. My children, think about it. Why would I send My Only Son to die for you to cause you harm? Why would I allow His blood to be shed to cause you defeat? Everything you want to carry, give it to Me. Everything that seems too big, give it to Me. Why tarry in your own understanding, with the things you don't understand? My yoke is easy, and My burden is light. Give it to Me.

My children, I AM here to tell you there are battles that you don't have to fight. There are wars you don't have to win, for I have already fought the fights and won the battles. Do not waste any more time fighting a war I have already won. Give it to Me, for I AM here, saith the Lord."

Matthew 11: 28 - 30 (MSG) - *"Are you tired? Worn out? Burned out on religion? Come to me. Get away with me and you'll recover your life. I'll show you how to take a real rest. Walk with me and work with me—watch how I do it. Learn the unforced rhythms of grace. I won't lay anything heavy or ill-fitting on you. Keep company with me and you'll learn to live freely and lightly."*

1 Peter 5 : 7 (NKJV) - *"casting all your care upon Him, for He cares for you."*

NOTES

What revelation did you receive from this BAM?

_____
_____
_____
_____
_____

What battles have you been fighting on your own? Have you learned to cast your cares on the Lord?

_____
_____
_____
_____
_____

Describe a time when you had to cast your cares unto the Lord.

_____
_____
_____
_____
_____

NOTES

IT'S MY BILL

(Don't Worry, Don't Try To Figure It Out)

''My children, I am leading you into unknown territory for the plan I have for you. My Purpose for you will require My Provision. It is My bill. Your faith wavers when you think that it is your bill. Everything you will need is in Me. Let belief and faith be in you, saith the Lord. I will cause provision in everything you do, according to My Purpose, according to the plan I have for you. Your obedience redeems the voucher of My Provision. Do not worry or get discouraged, for I will provide for My Will in your life through your obedience, your faith and belief. Do not take on the burden of trying to figure it out, for it has already been done. There is nothing that has not been planned out for you, saith the Lord. My children, Why do you worry about someone else's bill, when you are not the one who has to pay it?

Your purpose, My Plan is settled and ready; it is done. Do not worry. Do not be concerned with how provision will come when you are in My Will. It is My bill that has already been paid for, saith the Lord. Get out of the way trying to figure Me out. Trust Me. It is done, saith the Lord.

My children, why doubt Me? Have you checked My receipts? Have you read what I have already done in My Word? I AM the same today, yesterday and forever more. Do not worry. I will not lead you or ask you to follow Me where there is no provision, saith the Lord. Continue in your faith.

Let your faith move continuously. Continue to work your faith, for I have already paid the bill."

Philippians 4 : 19 (ESV) - *"And my God will supply every need of yours according to his riches in glory in Christ Jesus."*

Deuteronomy 28 : 1 - 3 (ESV) - *"And if you faithfully obey the voice of the LORD your God, being careful to do all his commandments that I command you today, the LORD your God will set you high above all the nations of the earth. And all these blessings shall come upon you and overtake you, if you obey the voice of the LORD your God. Blessed shall you be in the city, and blessed shall you be in the field."*

Luke 12 : 24 (ESV) - *"Consider the ravens: they neither sow nor reap, they have neither storehouse nor barn, and yet God feeds them. Of how much more value are you than the birds!"*

NOTES

What revelation did you receive from this BAM?

_____

_____

_____

_____

_____

What are some things you are trusting God to provide?

_____

_____

_____

_____

_____

Did your perspective on His Provision change after reading this BAM?

_____

_____

_____

_____

_____

NOTES

OUTWEIGH THE WAIT
(Wait on God)

''My children, the *weight* that the enemy has laid on you has outweighed your *wait* on Me. Some of My children have allowed the weight, the heaviness of this world, to get them distracted from waiting on Me. You have been consumed with the thoughts of this world, consumed with the weight of this world; it is turning you away from spending time with Me. It is distracting you from getting My instruction for your next move, saith the Lord.

My children, the difference between the *''weight''* and *''wait''* is that one must be lifted and the other requires My patience, but in both of them, you will need My help. My children, do not allow the wrong wait to weigh you down. There is freedom in your waiting and trusting Me. Do not allow the weight of this world to distract you and hold you back from what I have for you. My children, this is a correction that must be made quickly in your life. There is no time to waste. No time to allow the heaviness of this world to distract you. Remember what I have spoken and keep your eyes on Me. I AM at work, saith the Lord.''

JJ: *If the enemy can weigh you down, he will hold you down.*

Isaiah 40 : 31 (ESV) - *"but they who wait for the L*ORD *shall renew their strength; they shall mount up with wings like eagles; they shall run and not be weary; they shall walk and not faint.*

Psalm 130 : 5 (NKJV) - *"I wait for the L*ORD*, my soul waits, And in His word I do hope."*

Colossians 3 : 2 (ESV) - *"Set your minds on things that are above, not on things that are on earth."*

NOTES

What revelation did you receive from this BAM?

_____
_____
_____
_____
_____

Describe the difference between "wait" and "weight".

_____
_____
_____
_____
_____

What are some things you are waiting on God for? How can you shift your focus from distractions to wait on God?

_____
_____
_____
_____
_____

NOTES

WHAT YOU SEE VS WHAT I SAY
(God's Word is Truth)

''My children, know what I say in My Word, so you may not be deceived, deceived by what you see in this world. Too many of My children are being deceived by what they see and not listening to what I say. My children, what I say in My Word is the only Truth. Remain in My Truth, saith the Lord. You are in a time of serious deception and warfare. The spirit of conversion is among you and it is here to deceive you. Do not be deceived by the words of the enemy. My Truth, My Word is the only word that you stand on and live by, saith the Lord.

My children, there is only one way to Heaven. It is through My Son. There is only one way to Truth, it is through My Word. Do not be deceived by what you see or hear in this world. Know My Word, and you will not get caught by the hands of the enemy. Know My Truth, and you will not get caught by the spirit of conversion and deception.

My children, I warn you this day to know My Truth; the only Truth that sets you free. Do not allow the spirit of conversion to deceive you into compromising My Word. For if you compromise My Word, you compromise Me. If you compromise Me, you are deceived by the enemy, saith the Lord.

My children, know My Word, for My Word is your truth. My Word is your weapon. My Word gives you insight to what is happening in this world.

My children, when you know My Word, you know My Truth. When you know My Word, you know the Truth. Do not be moved by what you see or hear, but stand in My Word; stand on My Truth, saith the Lord.''

Conversion - *The fact of changing one's religion or beliefs or the act of persuading someone else to change theirs*

Romans 16 : 17 - 18 (ESV) - *''I appeal to you, brothers, to watch out for those who cause divisions and create obstacles contrary to the doctrine that you have been taught; avoid them. For such persons do not serve our Lord Christ, but their own appetites, and by smooth talk and flattery they deceive the hearts of the naive.''*

Ephesians 5 : 6 (ESV) - *''Let no one deceive you with empty words, for because of these things the wrath of God comes upon the sons of disobedience.''*

NOTES

What revelation did you receive from this BAM?

_____
_____
_____
_____
_____

In this time of deception and spiritual warfare, how can you stand on God's Truth?

_____
_____
_____
_____
_____

How do you discern the truth of God's Word in your life?

_____
_____
_____
_____
_____

NOTES

ROLLOVER

(Financial Blessings From Generation to Generation)

"My children will experience a rollover, a financial rollover, saith the Lord. I am rolling over generational blessings that have been stored up for My children, stored up for a time of release. I am rolling those blessings over to My children who have been obedient, rolling them over to My children who have taken the time to seek My Face and obey My Word. There will be supernatural blessings poured upon My children in these last days: blessings that will glorify Me, blessings that will define who I AM in their lives, undeniable blessings. There will be no greed in their heart and no sorrow in their spirit. They will be filled with the knowledge of who I AM and who has blessed them.

My children, the time of the rollover, the overflow is here. Never think that My Overflow is no longer here. Never think that it has passed you by, for it is here; here at this time to receive, saith the Lord. Do not miss it, but receive it through your faith and obedience, saith the Lord.

My children, the definition of My Rollover is abundance being poured on you: abundance to cover every part of your life, abundance for a purpose. It is a part of My Plan, saith the Lord."

Ephesians 3 : 20 - 21 (ESV) *- ''Now to him who is able to do far more abundantly than all that we ask or think, according to the power at work within us, to him be glory in the church and in Christ Jesus throughout all generations, forever and ever. Amen.''*

Proverbs 13 : 22 (ESV) *- ''A good man leaves an inheritance to his children's children, but the sinner's wealth is laid up for the righteous.''*

Jeremiah 29 : 11 (NIV) *- ''For I know the plans I have for you," declares the* L*ORD, "plans to prosper you and not to harm you, plans to give you hope and a future.''*

NOTES

What revelation did you receive from this BAM?

_____
_____
_____
_____
_____

How can you rest in faith and obedience to receive your financial rollover?

_____
_____
_____
_____
_____

What scriptures can you use to declare and decree your financial rollover?

_____
_____
_____
_____
_____

NOTES

MY TEACHINGS

(Don't Forget My Teachings)

"My children, don't forget My Teachings. I have outlined the things that you need in My Word. Do not run from My Teachings, for they will pave the way for you; pave the way to your finish line. Do not close your mouth to My Teachings. Open up your mouth, so that My Words may speak through you. Do not battle with My Teachings, for the fight has already been won. My children, do not run away from My Teachings. Run with them, for they will run with you, saith the Lord.

My children, My children, do not ignore My Teachings and do not hide from My Presence; for I am sending you fresh manna to be eaten, not to be ignored, but to fill you in areas that you are empty. You must remain in My Presence. You must remain in Me, saith the Lord."

---

2 Timothy 3 : 16 (ESV) - "All Scripture is breathed out by God and profitable for teaching, for reproof, for correction, and for training in righteousness,"

Psalms 143 : 10 (NKJV) - "Teach me to do Your will, for You are my God; Your Spirit is good. Lead me in the land of uprightness."

John 15 : 7 (ERV) - *"Stay joined together with me, and follow my teachings. If you do this, you can ask for anything you want, and it will be given to you."*

Psalm 32 : 8 (AMP) - *"I will instruct you and teach you in the way you should go; I will counsel you [who are willing to learn] with My eye upon you."*

NOTES

What revelation did you receive from this BAM?

_____
_____
_____
_____
_____

What has God been teaching you in this season?

_____
_____
_____
_____
_____

Describe a teaching from God that has changed your life.

_____
_____
_____
_____
_____

Bold Amazing Message From God

NOTES

WAR OF WORDS

(What You Speak)

"My children, there is a war of words happening in your life: words of wisdom vs words of fear. Do not allow fear to enter into your spirit. Do not allow fear to come out of your mouth. It will be what you speak that will validate what I will do in your life, saith the Lord. The enemy has no authority in My Words, but he will have them in yours when you speak in the spirit of negativity, when you speak twisted words to fit his plan. My children, speak only My Words and stand in My Truth, saith the Lord.

The enemy is trying to deceive you with twisted words and twisted thoughts. They hold no ground. My Word is the only word that you can stand on. It is your true foundation, saith the Lord. The enemy is twisting My Word to fit his plan. He is deceiving My children with twisted words and twisted thoughts, warring against the Truth, saith the Lord. Do not allow twisted words to deceive you. Stand in My Word and on My Word. Stand in My Truth, saith the Lord."

---

2 Timothy 1 : 7 (ESV) *- "for God gave us a spirit not of fear but of power and love and self-control."*

Matthew 15 : 11 (ESV) *- "it is not what goes into the mouth that defiles a person, but what comes out of the mouth; this defiles a person."*

Ephesians 4 : 29 (NIV) *- "Do not let any unwholesome talk come out of your mouths, but only what is helpful for building others up according to their needs, that it may benefit those who listen."*

Psalm 19 : 14 (ESV) *- "Let the words of my mouth and the meditation of my heart be acceptable in your sight, O LORD, my rock and my redeemer."*

NOTES

What revelation did you receive from this BAM?

_____
_____
_____
_____
_____

Have you been giving the enemy authority over your words? How have the enemy's negative words affected your life?

_____
_____
_____
_____
_____

Do you believe that the powerful Word of God will transform your life? What can you do to align your words with the Word of God?

_____
_____
_____
_____
_____

NOTES

COVER THE TABLE

(I Prepared The Table You Will Serve From)

"My children, the table is prepared for you. Only sit at the table that I will seat you, saith the Lord. You have everything you need to cover that table. You have everything you need to eat at the table. You do not have to worry about what you will eat, for I have already prepared everything that I have for you at the table. Sit only at the tables I will seat you, for there will be some tables that will not deserve your presence. My children, the anointing that I have over your life will bring change to the table. The tables I will seat you at, will cause change in the lives of others, for My Presence will be there. Cover the table, saith the Lord."

JJ's VISION : *I heard the Lord say "Cover The Table." Then I saw a big brown round table and someone sat down and pulled the chair up. As I was looking, I saw that there was nothing on it; the table was empty. Then I heard God say, "Cover The Table" and all of a sudden, a pure white table cloth came over the table. Fine plates and silverware started to appear: forks, spoons and knives. They were beautiful, simply indescribable. Everything that person needed was on the table. Suddenly, out of the corner of my right eye, I saw a tall man, but I did not see his face. He was wearing a black butler suit and over his arm, was a white towel. The* *white towel caught my attention because of how white the towel was; it was pure white. The tall man walked up and stood by the table. Then I heard the Lord say these words in my spirit, "A Servant's Heart." I asked God, "What do you mean when you say 'A Servant's Heart?'" "You must have a servant's heart, saith the Lord."*

''Everything you need is on the table. I am pulling you up to the table and you will eat from this table, saith the Lord. For I am here to serve you, but from this table, you will have to serve others. A Servant's Heart. You must have a servant's heart, saith the Lord. I am sitting you at the table that did not have anything on it, until you sat there, and because you are moving in My Will, My Purpose and Plan, and because you have obeyed Me, I will fill the table with everything that you need and much more, saith the Lord. Because you are My chosen ones, I have prepared a table for you. You will sit at the table, and I will fill it with everything that you need and I will be right there to serve you, but I need you to have a servant's heart. For when you sit at the table that I prepared for you, you are not only there to eat but to serve others. Cover the table, saith the Lord.

I have prepared a table for you. The table you sit at is the table you will serve at, saith the Lord.

My children, I am here to serve you, but I want you to have a servant's heart to serve others. Unless you have a servant's heart, you will not be good to those that persecute you. Unless you have a servant's heart, you will not bless those that talk about you. Unless you have a servant's heart, you will not forgive others as I have forgiven you, saith the Lord. Cover the table.

I will prepare a table for you, even in the presence of your enemies. But when I tell you to serve your enemies from that table, unless you have a servant's heart, you will not serve them. When I tell you to love your enemies from that table, unless you have a servant's heart, you will not love them. I need you to serve them with a servant's heart. Unless you have a servant's heart, you will not feed your enemies; you will not serve those who talk about you. My children, when you are serving others, you are serving Me. I am sitting you at tables not only to eat, but to serve Me.''

Psalms 23 : 5 (ESV) - *''You prepare a table before me in the presence of my enemies; you anoint my head with oil; my cup overflows.*

Luke 6 : 27 (ESV) - *''But I say to you who hear, Love your enemies, do good to those who hate you, bless those who curse you, pray for those who abuse you.''*

1 Peter 4 : 10 (ESV) - *''As each has received a gift, use it to serve one another, as good stewards of God's varied grace''*

Mark 10 : 45 (ESV) - *''For even the Son of Man came not to be served but to serve, and to give his life as a ransom for many.''*

NOTES

What revelation did you receive from this BAM?

_____
_____
_____
_____
_____

What does it mean to have a servant's heart?

_____
_____
_____
_____
_____

Did your perspective on ''You prepare a table before me in the presence of my enemies'' change after reading this BAM? How do you feel about having to serve your enemies?

_____
_____
_____
_____
_____

NOTES

PURPOSE NOT MAGIC

(God Is Not A Magic Trick)

''I am waiting for My children to move in their purpose, saith the Lord. I am waiting for My children to move with purpose, saith the Lord. So many of My children are waiting for things to happen without moving. Your faith requires movement, but you are not moving, saith the Lord. When you move in your faith, it brings forth miracles. Stop waiting on things to happen, as if you are waiting on magic; faith and belief are not magic and I am not your magician. I AM God. Quit waiting for magic tricks before you move into your purpose. Move with your faith and belief. Move with urgency into your purpose, saith the Lord. Do not be afraid. Do not be content in doing nothing, living outside of your purpose, waiting for things to happen. The wait is over My children. Stop waiting for Me to do magic and let your faith bring forth miracles. The Miracles are the evidence that your faith is real, that I AM real, saith the Lord. Move with faith and belief and move into your purpose, saith the Lord. I AM waiting for you to move in your purpose.''

Hebrews 11 : 1 (NKJV) - *''Now faith is the substance of things hoped for, the evidence of things not seen.''*

James 2 : 26 (ERV) - *''A person's body that does not have a spirit is dead. It is the same with faith—faith that does nothing is dead!''*

NOTES

What revelation did you receive from this BAM?

_____
_____
_____
_____
_____

Has anything hindered you from moving forward in your purpose? How can you move forward in faith?

_____
_____
_____
_____
_____

Have you ever thought about your faith bringing forth miracles? What miracles can you receive through your faith?

_____
_____
_____
_____
_____

NOTES

HOPE IN GLORY

(You Are No Longer Enthusiastic About God)

"My child, you have lost your hope in My Glory. You are no longer enthusiastic about what My Words say about you or to you. You have lost the sparkle of My Glory. You have laid down your weapons to fight no more. You have cried tears of defeat because your hope was no longer in Me. Why? Why My child, have you lost hope in My Glory? Why do you struggle within yourself of who I AM?

My child, I see your feelings and your emotions. I hear you cry. I was there when your hope fell to the ground and when your spirit became dry. I was there when you were tired and gave up hope in My Glory.

My child, My Love for you is massive. It is one of the most loving things you can have or feel. Hope in Glory. I would never put down My Love for you. I will never not see you as wonderfully made. I will never turn My Back on you and I will never lose Hope in you. My child, your hope in Me glorifies Me. Your faith in Me causes My Spirit to move with Joy. Your faith and belief in Me causes My Spirit to move mountains on your behalf. Your trust in Me causes Me to show up strong in your life. Your love for Me allows the space in your heart to be filled with My Love. Your faith in Me will never let you down, hope in My Glory. My child, you have put your hope down. You have put Me down, but when you put Me down, I picked you up because My Hope in you is for everlasting. My Faith in you will never change.

My child, never lose your hope. Never allow fear and disappointments to strip you of the very things you hope for. I gave you hope. It is yours to keep, saith the Lord. Oh, My child, I AM speaking to you because I love you. My Heart hurts when you lose hope. Keep your faith in Me. I have hope in you. I believe in you, My child. I AM here. Your hope in My Glory will never let you down, saith the Lord. When you lose hope, you lose spiritual life inside of you. Your spirit man can die because there is nothing to believe in, nothing to hope for and no faith to be found.''

Hope - A feeling of expectation, A desire for a certain thing to happen, A feeling of trust

---

Hebrews 11 : 1 (NKJV) - ''Now faith is the substance of things hoped for, the evidence of things not seen.''

Romans 15 : 13 (NIV) *- ''May the God of hope fill you with all joy and peace as you trust in him, so that you may overflow with hope by the power of the Holy Spirit.''*

Isaiah 40 : 31 (NIV) *- ''but those who hope in the* L ORD *will renew their strength. They will soar on wings like eagles; they will run and not grow weary, they will walk and not be faint.''*

NOTES

What revelation did you receive from this BAM?

_____
_____
_____
_____
_____

Describe a time when your hope in God might have fallen. How did God help you pick it back up?

_____
_____
_____
_____
_____

How does it feel to know that God has hope in you?

_____
_____
_____
_____
_____

NOTES

HAIRLINE

(The Line To Receive And Not To Receive Is Thin)

"There is a very thin line to receive and not to receive. My children, My Time is drawing near. The time has come when the line that was once wide is now thin. It has become a hairline. I am coming to bring you this word, so that you may know how close it is to you receiving or not receiving. It is according to what you surrender to Me. You have not surrendered your all to Me. I have called you to move forward, but yet you stay. I have called you to get in My Presence, but yet I AM not on your time schedule. My children, the time has come to draw near to Me, to move quickly in My Presence and through My Spirit, saith the Lord. Time is passing by you. It is time to surrender your all to Me. The more time passes, the thinner the line gets. The time to receive or not receive is closing in on you, saith the Lord."

Hairline - A very thin fine line

Ecclesiastes 3 : 1 - 4 (ERV) - *"There is a right time for everything, and everything on earth will happen at the right time. There is a time to be born and a time to die. There is a time to plant and a time to pull up plants. There is a time to kill and a time to heal. There is a time to destroy and a time to build. There is a time to cry and a time to laugh."*

Matthew 7 : 14 (ESV) - *"For the gate is narrow and the way is hard that leads to life, and those who find it are few."*

NOTES

What revelation did you receive from this BAM?

_____
_____
_____
_____
_____

What can you do to spend more time in the Lord's Presence?

_____
_____
_____
_____
_____

What can you do to be on the receiving side of the hairline?

_____
_____
_____
_____
_____

NOTES

REASSEMBLE

(God Will Put Us Back Together)

"Many of My children are not broken, but they need to be reassembled. They are scattered amongst themselves. They are running in different directions, running alone, instead of running together. They are not broken, but divided, separated. They are not lost, but divided, separated. It is time to reassemble My Body. Reassemble My Body and move forward. My children, I call you this day to not tarry alongside each other, but to come together in unity. Unity in the Body. I AM calling you not to separate or stay divided, but to come back together again. My children, the enemy has worked hard to divide the Body because of the strength in the Body. There is strength in the whole Body. The strength in the Body is what you need. Pray for the Body. Pray for My Body; that you will all obey My Word and come together. Come together in unity, in wholeness. My children, each of you can play a part in reassembling My Body, through your obedience and through the purpose I have given you. My children, reassemble My Body. Come back together. Come back together in prayer and thanksgiving, saith the Lord. For the time is now for the Body to be whole, saith the Lord. It is time for you to come together. Everyone has an assignment and everyone can help reassemble My Body."

Reassemble - To gather together again, To bring or put together the parts again, To come together, Rejoin, Reunite

---

1 Corinthians 12 : 14 (NIRV) - "So the body is not made up of just one part. It has many parts."

Ephesians 4 : 16 (ERV) - "and the whole body depends on him. All the parts of the body are joined and held together, with each part doing its own work. This causes the whole body to grow and to be stronger in love."

1 Corinthians 12 : 21 - 22 (NIRV) - "The eye can't say to the hand, "I don't need you!" The head can't say to the feet, "I don't need you!" In fact, it is just the opposite."

1 Corinthians 12 : 26 - 27 (ESV) - "If one member suffers, all suffer together; if one member is honored, all rejoice together. Now you are the body of Christ and individually members of it."

NOTES

What revelation did you receive from this BAM?

_____
_____
_____
_____
_____

What are some things you can do to bring unity to The Body of Christ?

_____
_____
_____
_____
_____

What can The Body of Christ accomplish when operating in unity and wholeness?

_____
_____
_____
_____
_____

NOTES

RAISE YOUR SHIELD

(Raise Your Shield of Faith)

"No more time My children. No more time. Raise your shield. Remain in your faith. There is no more time to be faithless. Raise your shield. Remain in Faith. My children, the enemy is waging war on your faith. Raise your shield against the enemy. Stand in Faith, saith the Lord."

Ephesians 6 : 10 - 12 (ESV) - *"Finally, be strong in the Lord and in the strength of his might. Put on the whole armor of God, that you may be able to stand against the schemes of the devil. For we do not wrestle against flesh and blood, but against the rulers, against the authorities, against the cosmic powers over this present darkness, against the spiritual forces of evil in the heavenly places."*

Ephesians 6 : 16 (ERV) - *"And also use the shield of faith with which you can stop all the burning arrows that come from the Evil One"*

1 John 5 : 4 - 5 (ESV) - *"For everyone who has been born of God overcomes the world. And this is the victory that has overcome the world—our faith. Who is it that overcomes the world except the one who believes that Jesus is the Son of God?"*

2 Corinthians 10 : 4 (ESV) - *"For the weapons of our warfare are not of the flesh but have divine power to destroy strongholds."*

Romans 1 : 17 (ESV) - *"For in it the righteousness of God is revealed from faith for faith, as it is written, "The righteous shall live by faith.""*

Hebrews 11 : 6 (ESV) - *"And without faith it is impossible to please Him,"*

NOTES

What revelation did you receive from this BAM?

_____
_____
_____
_____
_____

How has the enemy waged war on your faith?

_____
_____
_____
_____
_____

How can you defeat the enemy?

_____
_____
_____
_____
_____

NOTES

HIDDEN TREASURE

(You Have Hidden Treasures Inside You)

"Your hidden treasures are yet to be found by you. The very treasures that I placed in you are priceless, unique, ready to be adorned. My children, you have treasures in you, but you are asking Me: 'What more could it be? What is inside of me? I do not feel it. I do not know what's in me. What does God have for me?'

You have treasures inside of you, saith the Lord. To find those treasures, you have to come into the knowledge of who I AM, saith the Lord. Then, you will find the treasures inside of you.

My children, I have placed gifts inside of you; gifts that you do not know. You must know the treasure I have placed in you, in order to use it for My Glory. You must come into the knowledge of who I AM through My Word and through being in My Presence, saith the Lord. My children, you are crying out to Me: 'What is it? What is in me?' Your question should now be 'Who is He that is in me?', saith the Lord. Come into the knowledge of who I AM, and I will reveal to you hidden secrets, hidden places, hidden promises and your hidden treasures. Come into the knowledge of who I AM, for what I have placed inside of you can no longer be hidden, saith the Lord. Come out of hiding and search your heart. The revealing of your treasures is now, saith the Lord. No longer allow the devil to hide your treasures from you by keeping you blind to who I AM and who you are in Me. Draw near to Me for the reveal is now, saith the Lord."

Matthew 6 : 21 (ESV) - *''For where your treasure is, there your heart will be also.''*

2 Corinthians 4 : 7 (ERV) - *''We have this treasure from God, but we are only like clay jars that hold the treasure. This is to show that the amazing power we have is from God, not from us.''*

NOTES

What revelation did you receive from this BAM?

_____

_____

_____

_____

How can you come into the knowledge of God, to know what gifts He has placed inside you?

_____

_____

_____

_____

_____

How can you use your gifts for God's Glory?

_____

_____

_____

_____

_____

NOTES

HEART OF A CARPENTER

(Help Build My Kingdom)

"I want My children to have a heart of a carpenter: ready to be used, used to help build My Kingdom. Build My Kingdom. My children, I have placed in you the skills and the anointing to build. I have given you the tools to use that will build you from the inside out: tools that would touch the lives of My children and turn their hearts back to Me. My children, I desire for you to have a heart of a carpenter; a heart that represents My Heart. A heart ready to build. A heart for My people. A humble heart. A heart that is ready to serve. My children, on this day, will you receive a heart of a carpenter? Will you help build My Kingdom? Do not be afraid. This world is now under construction, saith the Lord."

God, The Carpenter ~ Jesus, The Carpenter ~ Holy Spirit, The Carpenter

We are the carpenters

Mark 6 : 2 - 3 (ERV) - *"On the Sabbath day Jesus taught in the synagogue, and many people heard him. They were amazed and said, "Where did this man get this teaching? How did he get such wisdom? Who gave it to him? And where did he get the power to do miracles? Isn't he just the carpenter we know..."*

NOTES

What revelation did you receive from this BAM?

_____
_____
_____
_____
_____

How has God repaired your heart since you gave your life to Him?

_____
_____
_____
_____
_____

How can you help build The Kingdom of God with the heart of a carpenter?

_____
_____
_____
_____
_____

NOTES

HEART - ATTACKS

(Guard Your Heart)

"There have been attacks on your heart from the enemy, saith the Lord. Guard your hearts, saith the Lord. Your heart has been attacked because you did not know the importance of your heart; the importance of Who is at the center of your heart. My children, check your heart. Examine your heart. Your heart is so important to Me. Your heart is what you surrender to Me, saith the Lord.

There have been attacks on your heart, to stop you from going in the right direction; heart-attacks from the enemy, but where I am taking you, your heart must be right. Surrender your heart to Me, My children. The time is now to open up your heart to Me, to surrender your whole heart to Me, saith the Lord. Know the importance of the heart. Know how delicate it is, yet how strong it can be. Surrender your heart, your willing heart unto Me, saith the Lord. My children, the attacks from the enemy have left so many of your hearts feeling cold, empty, broken and wounded. Surrender your hearts to Me, saith the Lord. Where there is damage, I will repair it. Where there is loneliness, I will fill it, because I am here. Where there is loss of love, I will restore. Open up your heart and surrender to Me, for your heart is the place that I want to be, saith the Lord.

Proverbs 4 : 23 (NIV) - *"Above all else, guard your heart for everything you do flows from it."*

Jeremiah 29 : 13 (NIV) - *"You will seek me and find me when you seek me with all your heart."*

Psalm 51 : 10 (NIV) - *"Create in me a pure heart, O God, and renew a steadfast spirit within me."*

Proverbs 3 : 5 (NKJV) - *"Trust in the LORD with all your heart, And lean not on your own understanding"*

Matthew 22 : 30 (NKJV) - *"Jesus said to him, "'You shall love the LORD your God with all your heart, with all your soul, and with all your mind."*

Ezekiel 36 : 26 (MSG) - *"I'll give you a new heart, put a new spirit in you. I'll remove the stone heart from your body and replace it with a heart that's God-willed, not self-willed."*

NOTES

What revelation did you receive from this BAM?

_____
_____
_____
_____
_____

Have you surrendered your whole heart to God? How can you continue to surrender your heart to the Lord?

_____
_____
_____
_____
_____

What attacks of the heart have the Lord helped you overcome?

_____
_____
_____
_____
_____

NOTES

FIGHT

(Fight For What God Has For You)

"Fight. My children, fight. Fight with the very thing I have given you: My Word. It is your weapon. Open up your mouth and fight. A person who is silent does not speak; a person who does not speak can not proclaim My Word out loud. Fight. Fight using My Words. Speak My Word, saith the Lord.

For so long, My children have been quiet and beat down by the enemy because they did not know that they can use My Word to fight against their enemy. My children, grab hold of My Word and fight. Grab hold of the weapon that I have given you and fight against your enemy. Do not allow your enemy to steal from you or to take from you. Use My Word and fight, saith the Lord. Fight for what is already yours. Fight for the dreams that I have given you. Fight for the vision I have shown you. Do not allow the enemy to steal the vision and purpose that is inside of you, saith the Lord. There's a fight around you, but the weapon is in you. Fight with My Word, saith the Lord. My children, pick up your weapon and fight."

Deuteronomy 20 : 4 (NIV) - *"For the LORD your God is the one who goes with you to fight for you against your enemies to give you victory."*

Deuteronomy 3 : 22 (ESV) - *''You shall not fear them, for it is the LORD your God who fights for you.''*

Luke 4 : 8 (NKJV) - *''And Jesus answered and said to him, "Get behind Me, Satan! For it is written, 'You shall worship the LORD your God, and Him only you shall serve.' ''*

Ephesians 6 : 10 - 11 (ESV) - *''Finally, be strong in the Lord and in the strength of his might. Put on the whole armor of God, that you may be able to stand against the schemes of the devil.*

Ephesians 6 : 17 (ESV) - *''and take the helmet of salvation, and the sword of the Spirit, which is the word of God''*

NOTES

What revelation did you receive from this BAM?

_____
_____
_____
_____
_____

Have you ever thought of God's Word as a weapon to fight against the enemy? What other weapons of God are you aware of?

_____
_____
_____
_____
_____

How can you use God's Word to fight against the enemy? List 3 scriptures that you will use to fight against the enemy.

_____
_____
_____
_____
_____

NOTES

THERE IS A SHIFT
(And It Will Be Uncomfortable)

''Your position is important. Where I am taking you and leading you will cause some things to fall from you, saith the Lord. This shift will cause you to be uncomfortable. It will cause you to question yourself and My Will for your life. Be not dismayed; for I am positioning you for your purpose. I am positioning you to stand out in the middle of the crowd, saith the Lord. I have called for repentance to clear the way for positioning. I am calling for My children to move in the right direction in their life. I am calling for you to about face; to turn away from everything that is not of Me, to move in the right direction, saith the Lord. I am directing you and positioning you. I am placing you in the right place. For some, it will not be easy. For you, it will be uncomfortable, but it is necessary. My children, the shift in your life is repositioning you to go in the right direction. Move in Me and with Me. It is a part of the plan that I have for you. Do not question the shift. Do not question the repositioning, any longer; for I am moving you. Follow Me. Follow your leader, saith the Lord. Follow Me. Follow My Plan; follow My Direction and you will always go the right way, saith the Lord.''

About Face - The act of turning to face the opposite direction, Turn around

Shift - To move or cause to move from one place to another, To rearrange, To reposition

---

Isaiah 43 : 18 - 19 (ESV) - ''Remember not the former things, nor consider the things of old. Behold, I am doing a new thing; now it springs forth, do you not perceive it? I will make a way in the wilderness and rivers in the desert.''

NOTES

What revelation did you receive from this BAM?

_____
_____
_____
_____
_____

What has God shifted in your life? What changes did you have to make in the shift?

_____
_____
_____
_____
_____

Has God revealed where He is positioning you? Did it make you uncomfortable? How can you prepare for the repositioning?

_____
_____
_____
_____
_____

NOTES

GO! POSSESS IT!

(Take Ownership)

''My children, it is one thing to accept My Will and another thing to possess what is in My Will. I do not want My children to just sit in My Will, but to move in My Will, saith the Lord. My children, the work is not finished because you have accepted My Will. It is not finished until you possess what is in My Will. My children, it is time to possess it, to take ownership of what is already yours, saith the Lord. My children, My Word is true. My Promises are true. They are all for you. Now Go! Move! Take possession of what is in My Hand, saith the Lord. Be courageous. Take possession of My Will, for it is yours, saith the Lord.''

G.O. - God's Obedience

Possess - To Have, To Hold, To Own

Joshua 1 : 1 - 9 (ERV) - *''Moses was the LORD's servant, and Joshua son of Nun was Moses' helper. After Moses died, the LORD spoke to Joshua and said, "My servant Moses is dead. Now you and all these people must go across the Jordan River. You must go into the land I am giving to the Israelites.*

Joshua 1 : 9 (NIV) *- "Have I not commanded you? Be strong and courageous. Do not be afraid; do not be discouraged, for the LORD your God will be with you wherever you go."*

Numbers 33 : 53 (NIV) *- "Take possession of the land and settle in it, for I have given you the land to possess."*

Deuteronomy 1 : 8 (ESV) *- "See, I have set the land before you. Go in and take possession of the land that the LORD swore to your fathers, to Abraham, to Isaac, and to Jacob, to give to them and to their offspring after them."*

Deuteronomy 30 : 5 (ESV) *- "And the LORD your God will bring you into the land that your fathers possessed, that you may possess it. And he will make you more prosperous and numerous than your fathers."*

NOTES

What revelation did you receive from this BAM?

_____
_____
_____
_____
_____

What does it mean to go and possess God's Will for your life?

_____
_____
_____
_____
_____

God said, "Take ownership of what is already yours." What are some things that are already yours? How can you go and possess it?

_____
_____
_____
_____
_____

NOTES

HOUSE OF PRAYER

(Direct Communication To God)

''Your house should be a house of prayer. My children, your prayers are a direct line of communication to Me. It is time to pray. So many of you did not think that your prayers would be answered. You felt you did not know how to pray. Prayer is a doorbell to Heaven. Prayer allows things to change in your life. Prayer is more powerful than you know, more simpler than you think and clearer than you can see. Prayer is a pathway to Me. Do not take praying for granted, saith the Lord, for you are communicating with Me. So many of My children have been discouraged in their prayer life because you felt your prayers would not be answered. Some have questioned whether I even heard their prayers. I AM the One who hears your prayers, saith the Lord.

My children, it is time for your house to pray; prayer is essential and necessary in your life. I am calling you to be a house of prayer; praying for yourself and others, praying that My Will be done in your life and in the lives of others. My children, prayer is your weapon to use to counterattack against your enemies. Do not have fear when you pray. Do not fear to pray. Do not allow anyone to confuse you about prayer. Prayer is a direct line of communication to Me. Stand in your faith and belief when you pray.

My children, I am calling for you to be a house of prayer, to declare My Word when you pray. Prayer brings life in the spiritual realm that manifests in the natural. Declare My Word when you pray. Be the house that prays, saith the Lord.''

---

1 Thessalonians 5 : 17 (ESV) - *''Pray without ceasing,''*

Colossians 4 : 2 (ESV) - *''Continue steadfastly in prayer, being watchful in it with thanksgiving.''*

Philippians 4 : 6 - 7 (NIV) - *''Do not be anxious about anything, but in every situation, by prayer and petition, with thanksgiving, present your requests to God. And the peace of God, which transcends all understanding, will guard your hearts and your minds in Christ Jesus.''*

Matthew 6 : 9 - 13 (NKJV) - *''In this manner, therefore, pray: Our Father in heaven, Hallowed be Your name. Your kingdom come. Your will be done on earth as it is in heaven. Give us this day our daily bread. And forgive us our debts, As we forgive our debtors. And do not lead us into temptation, but deliver us from the evil one. For Yours is the kingdom and the power and the glory forever. Amen.''*

NOTES

What revelation did you receive from this BAM?

_____
_____
_____
_____
_____

How important is prayer to you? What does your prayer life look like?

_____
_____
_____
_____
_____

How can you strengthen your prayer life?

_____
_____
_____
_____
_____

NOTES

BACKSTEPS WILL NEVER MOVE YOU FORWARD
(Don't Go Back Into Sin)

"Too many times My children have asked for forgiveness from their sins, sins that caused their spirit to grieve. I forgave you for these sins and transgressions to only find you going back, indulging in the same sins, transgressions, mishaps, defiance, reckless behaviors; but yet, your sins are forgiven over and over again. My children, backsteps will never move you forward to the place I have for you. Do you believe Me? Do you believe My Word: the wages of sin is death? So, why My children, do you allow the foul spirits of the air to reverse you, to turn you away from Me when I have forgiven you. Why do you go back to sin? I want you to move forward and away from all the things that will cause you harm and spiritual death; things that will cause you to walk backwards from Me, to walk away from the plan that I have for you. My children, I would rather for you to stand in one place seeking Me, than to step backwards and away from your relationship with Me. My children, do you believe that sin will never move you forward in Me, saith the Lord? My children, move forward in My Promises. Move forward in Me. Going backwards will only cause a spirit of rebellion to fall upon you. Move forward in My Forgiveness. Move forward in the love that you have for Me. Go and sin no more, saith the Lord."

Romans 6 : 23 (ESV) - *"For the wages of sin is death, but the free gift of God is eternal life in Christ Jesus our Lord."*

1 John 1 : 19 (ESV) - *"If we confess our sins, he is faithful and just to forgive us our sins and to cleanse us from all unrighteousness."*

NOTES

What revelation did you receive from this BAM?

_____

_____

_____

_____

_____

What does "Go and sin no more" mean to you?

_____

_____

_____

_____

_____

How can you take heed to this correction and not sin against God?

_____

_____

_____

_____

_____

NOTES

THE CATCHER AND THE THIEF
(The Enemy Can Steal Your Words)

"My children, the enemy is there to capture your words and steal your dreams; to steal the plans I have for you. Only through your words, your deeds, fear and doubt, can he steal it from you. Speaking negative words gives the enemy access to you, to capture you. My children, the words you speak out of your mouth will reflect what will happen in your life. No longer speak the enemy's language. Speak My Word. Speak My Truth, saith the Lord. Separate yourself from doubtful words: words that were meant to kill and destroy you, words that will not fill you, saith the Lord.

My children, speak only life. No longer allow negative words to kill what is inside of you, to take away what is for you. My children, the enemy catches your words and uses them to harm you. Guard your mouth from negative words. Guard your tongue from negative speaking. Watch the words that come out of your mouth. The words that you speak represent your faith and belief, saith the Lord. It reflects your heart. When My Word is in your heart, life will come out of your mouth."

JJ's VISION: A baseball game. The object of the game is to make it home, to get to home base. Your mouth is the ball. There are angels in the outfield ready to help you make it to home base. The enemy is there to catch your ball, to catch your words, to prevent you from making it home. He watches your words when they come out of your mouth. Your words activate the angels in the outfield, or they activate the enemy, who slides in and catches your words, to stop you from getting to home base. But your words of faith, knock it out of the park. HOME RUN.

Proverbs 18 : 21 (NKJV) - *"Death and life are in the power of the tongue, And those who love it will eat its fruit."*

Proverbs 4 : 23 (MSG) - *"Keep vigilant watch over your heart; that's where life starts. Don't talk out of both sides of your mouth; avoid careless banter, white lies, and gossip."*

Psalm 19 : 14 (NKJV) - *"Let the words of my mouth and the meditation of my heart be acceptable in Your sight, O LORD, my strength and my Redeemer."*

Proverbs 21 : 23 (ERV) - *"People who are careful about what they say will save themselves from trouble."*

NOTES

What revelation did you receive from this BAM?

_____
_____
_____
_____
_____

What kind of words have you been speaking? Have you been speaking words that can move your faith or stop your faith?

_____
_____
_____
_____
_____

Did the vision of the baseball game help you see how the enemy can grab a hold of your negative words? What words can you say to activate your angels in the outfield?

_____
_____
_____
_____
_____

NOTES

THE POWER OF DIVINE CONNECTIONS

"I am causing divine connections to rise up like never before. I am sitting you at tables that are already prepared for you. I am sending you into rooms where the walls have called you blessed. I am placing you in the right places with the right people. I am causing your purpose to flow through divine connections. I am joining you with true possibilities and no longer with people who don't believe in you, who do not believe in Me. I am causing My children to unite in the plans that I have for them, to further My Kingdom. I am sending My children into rooms, streets, boardrooms, houses, schools, restaurants, churches, communities, states and cities to connect with the ones that are divinely placed there. I am connecting you to your divine connections. I am connecting you to the ones who are connected to the Vine, to remain fruitful in My Kingdom. No longer My children, should you be willing to sit with the ones who do not believe I AM real, who do not believe what I put in you is real. I am placing you in areas where you can grow swiftly. This is the season for divine connections; know that I am sending you connections that will not spoil the vine, but to multiply the fruit for My Kingdom, saith the Lord."

Divine Connections - Relationships, Spiritually connected by God

John 15 : 4 (NIV) - *"Remain in me, as I also remain in you. No branch can bear fruit by itself; it must remain in the vine. Neither can you bear fruit unless you remain in me."*

Proverbs 27 : 17 (ESV) - *"Iron sharpens iron and one man sharpens another."*

Ecclesiastes 4 : 9 - 10 (NIV) - *"Two are better than one, because they have a good return for their labor: If either of them falls down, one can help the other up."*

NOTES

What revelation did you receive from this BAM?

_____
_____
_____
_____
_____

What understanding do you have about the purpose of divine connections? Are you prepared to receive your divine connections?

_____
_____
_____
_____
_____

How can you prepare yourself to be someone else's divine connection?

_____
_____
_____
_____
_____

NOTES

READY OR NOT, HERE I COME
(Jesus Is Coming)

"My children, I AM coming. My time is not based on your time or your schedule. Do not miss the most important part of your journey in life, the part of knowing that I AM coming. I am preparing My children for My Return. The time is now to move in Me and with Me. Your choice to choose Me is crucial, crucial in these last days. I AM coming soon, saith the Lord.

My children, you have to believe that I AM coming. When you believe that I AM coming, you will prepare yourself for My Coming. Prepare yourself by living in your purpose, by using your gifts and talents for My Kingdom, by surrendering completely to Me, saith the Lord.

My children, the time is now to position yourself to be used and blessed by Me. I AM coming for My Church, but at this moment, I AM coming to tell you to move in your purpose, saith the Lord. I AM coming soon and My Time is not on your time. My Time is My Time. In order for you to be ready, you must believe that I AM coming soon, saith the Lord.

My children, your choice to be used by Me is your choice. The choice to be ready is your choice, but with or without you, it is happening.

Ready or not, I AM COMING.

I want to find you moving in your purpose, on the behalf of My Kingdom. The time to prepare for My Coming is now. The time to grow is now. The time to expand is now. The time to reverence Me is now. The time for blessings and miracles is now. The time to be aware is now. The time to move is now. The time to obey Me is now. The time to surrender to Me is now.

My children, ready or not, I AM COMING. Hesitation to prepare for My Coming will cost you. Your delays will rob you of the purpose that I have for you. Prepare for My Coming, saith the Lord.''

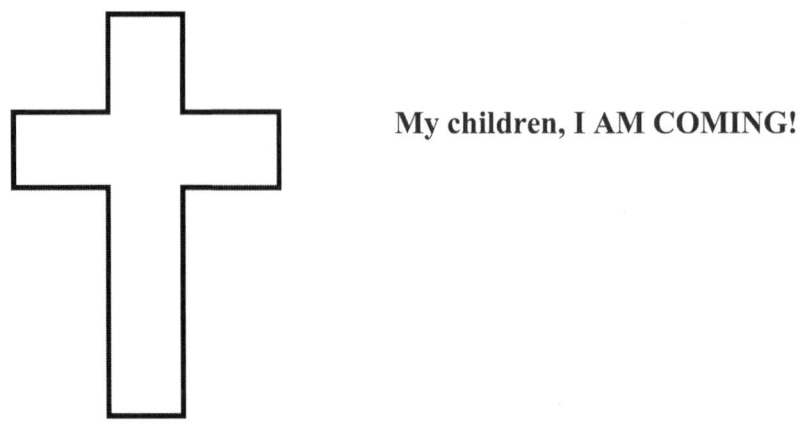

My children, I AM COMING!

Matthew 24 : 36 (NIV) - *''But about that day or hour no one knows, not even the angels in heaven, nor the Son, but only the Father.''*

NOTES

What revelation did you receive from this BAM?

_____
_____
_____
_____
_____

Will you be ready for when Jesus returns? How can you prepare for His Return?

_____
_____
_____
_____
_____

Will the Lord find you moving in your purpose or sitting on the sidelines? What things will the Lord find you doing? How can those things be used for His Kingdom?

_____
_____
_____
_____
_____

NOTES

I AM CLOSING DOORS

"My children, there are doors that must be closed in order for you to enter into the doors that are open to you, saith the Lord.

My children, your freedom to access the doors that I have for you depends on you. You must not be afraid to walk through the doors I have set before you, and you must not be afraid of the doors that I am closing. My children, I am now closing those doors that have been falsely opened to you: doors that were never supposed to be open, doors that have hindered you, doors that have locked you inside of yourself, to be a slave to self, saith the Lord. I am opening doors that only you can walk through. Do not be afraid to walk through them. Do not allow fear and doubt to stop you from walking into wide open doors of divine opportunities, saith the Lord. My children, rejoice for the doors that I am opening; rejoice for the doors that I am closing, saith the Lord."

Revelation 3 : 8 (ESV) - *" 'I know your works. Behold, I have set before you an open door, which no one is able to shut. I know that you have but little power, and yet you have kept my word and have not denied my name.'"*

NOTES

What revelation did you receive from this BAM?

_____
_____
_____
_____
_____

God opens and closes doors in our lives. Do you recognize the doors He has opened for you and the doors He has closed for you? What doors are you thankful for?

_____
_____
_____
_____
_____

How can you walk through God's open doors?

_____
_____
_____
_____
_____

NOTES

CHASING THE MIST

(The Cloud, The Fog, The Haze)

"My children, so many times in your life, you have chased after things. You have run after things that you felt you needed. Today I say to you, chase after Me, seek Me, search for Me, for I AM here. My children, stop chasing the mist in this world, the very things that will disappear right in front of you. This world's mist is designed to evaporate, to disappear, never to remain steady. You have covered your eyes to things that are real in Me, to seek things that gratify the flesh, not your spirit, saith the Lord. Have I not told you to seek Me first? Have I not told you in My Word to search for Me with all your heart, for I am here? My children, when you chase the mist, you cannot clearly see the vision I have for you. A mist is a fog that reduces visibility, which makes it hard for you to see. Stop chasing the mist. Stop running after things of no value. Know that everything that I have for you holds its own value and will not diminish or disappear, for I am with you. Believe it and I will show you, saith the Lord.

My children, do you want what I have for you? Ask Me to help you see the vision pass the mist. Ask Me to help you clearly see the vision that I have for you. No longer chase the mist. Chase after Me. A mist will disappear, but I will always remain, saith the Lord."

JJ's VISION: *God showed me a vision of the mist. It was a thick and deep fog. It was so thick, I could barely see through it. When I tried to reach for it, there was nothing really there. He revealed that this was the type of cloudy mist that we were chasing; things that blurred our vision; things that would disappear.*

Mist - A haze or film over the eyes and resulting in blurred vision, Fog, Prevent clear perception

---

Matthew 6 : 33 (ESV) - *"But seek first the kingdom of God and his righteousness, and all these things will be added to you."*

Jeremiah 29 : 13 (ESV) - *"You will seek me and find me, when you seek me with all your heart."*

NOTES

What revelation did you receive from this BAM?

_____
_____
_____
_____
_____

What misty things have you chased in your life? How did these things cloud your vision?

_____
_____
_____
_____
_____

How can you chase after God more?

_____
_____
_____
_____
_____

Bold Amazing Message From God

NOTES

WALKING STURDY

(Walk Steady)

"A steady walk is a renewed mind. My children, a renewed mind will help you walk sturdy and consistent in Me, saith the Lord. When your mind is not renewed, your spirit is weak. When your mind is renewed, your spirit is strong. Renewing your mind will cause you to walk sturdy in Me. When your mind is strong in Me, your walk is sturdy; walking upright in everything you do. My children, there is no weakness in My Mind and there shall be no weakness in yours. Stay strong in Me. Walk sturdy in Me, saith the Lord."

Sturdy - Strong, Well Built, Solid, Powerful, Tough, Mighty

Steady - Firmly Fixed, Balanced, Unshakeable

Romans 12 : 2 (ESV) - *"Do not be conformed to this world, but be transformed by the renewal of your mind"*

Ephesians 6 : 10 (MSG) - *"And that about wraps it up. God is strong, and he wants you strong."*

NOTES

What revelation did you receive from this BAM?

_____
_____
_____
_____
_____

Have you renewed your mind and taken on the mind of Christ? How can you renew your mind to make sure it is strong in the Lord?

_____
_____
_____
_____
_____

How can you be consistent in your walk with God?

_____
_____
_____
_____
_____

NOTES

GIVE ME PERMISSION
(Say Yes To God)

"My children, remove the ties that bind you and give Me permission to use you, saith the Lord. I will not force you to serve Me. I will not force you to be used by Me, but when you freely say 'Yes' to Me and obey Me, you are giving Me permission to pour My Promises upon your life, saith the Lord. My children, take yourself back to the day when you first asked Me to come into your heart. You gave Me permission to enter. Give Me permission now to use you for My Kingdom. Your 'Yes' to Me gives Me permission to say 'Yes' to you. Your complete surrender gives Me permission to surrender My all to you. My children, there will come a day soon when your permission will no longer be needed, but for now, I do not have your full permission, because you are holding on to things that are hindering you from saying 'Yes' to Me. When you release what's in your hand, I release what's in Mine. Give Me permission to use you. Say 'Yes',

saith the Lord."

---

2 Corinthians 1 : 20 (ESV) - *"For all the promises of God find their Yes in him. That is why it is through him that we utter our Amen to God for his glory."*

NOTES

What revelation did you receive from this BAM?

_____
_____
_____
_____

Have you said 'Yes' to God? What does it mean to give God permission to use you? What does that look like in your life?

_____
_____
_____
_____

How does it make you feel to know that your 'Yes' to God is a 'Yes' to you?

_____
_____
_____
_____

NOTES

PINPOINT IT

(Pinpoint Your Gifts and Talents)

"My children, it is time to pinpoint your gifts and talents. Many of My children are asking Me, 'What are my gifts, my talents, the purpose You have for me, Lord?' My children, pinpoint it. Take it back to the very thing that caused your spirit to smile. Pinpoint it; the very thing that caused you joy and peace, the very thing that honors Me. Pinpoint it. Think about it. Take yourself to your natural being, the things you do naturally with no effort. My children, your questions of, 'What are my gifts and talents?' are valid. I have given you all a gift, and talents inside of you. Pinpoint it. You have asked Me to show you. I am asking you to pinpoint what is already there. Write it down, so you may see it and feel it. What is it you like to do? My children, I will not give talents that are undesirable, but meaningful talents that were created just for you; gifts and talents that can be used by Me. My children, pinpoint the very things that I have put in you, the very thing that I called you to do. Within your gifts and talents, I have several ways for it to be used and millions of ways that your gift and talents will reach My children. Look inside; you will see. It is in you, saith the Lord."

Pinpoint - To locate, To discover, To identify, To recognize

James 1 : 17 (ESV) *- "Every good gift and every perfect gift is from above, coming down from the Father of lights, with whom there is no variation or shadow due to change."*

1 Corinthians 12 : 4 - 6 (ESV) *- "Now there are varieties of gifts, but the same Spirit; and there are varieties of service, but the same Lord; and there are varieties of activities, but it is the same God who empowers them all in everyone."*

Romans 11 : 29 (ESV) *- "For the gifts and the calling of God are irrevocable."*

Irrevocable *- Can not be changed or reversed*

NOTES

What revelation did you receive from this BAM?

_____
_____
_____
_____
_____

What things naturally come to you? What things do you naturally enjoy doing? Have you ever thought about those things being your gifts and talents?

_____
_____
_____
_____
_____

How can your gifts and talents be used for God's glory?

_____
_____
_____
_____
_____

NOTES

THE ABILITY TO DISCERN

(Ask For Discernment)

"Discernment brings clarity. Discernment is something that some of My children do not ask Me for. Discernment brings clarity to your surroundings. Discernment is real; it is a gift of My Spirit, saith the Lord. My children, having the ability to discern the very small things is advantageous to you. To discern My Presence will help you to discern the presence of the enemy, but you do not ask for discernment. Why do you not ask? My children, discernment is the very thing that brings clarity without speaking. Discernment gives you the advantage. My children, when you do not have discernment, you are easily misled through the flesh, saith the Lord.

For what is not discerned in the flesh is discerned in the spirit. When you are moving in My Spirit, there is discernment and awareness; it gives you the ability to see your enemy coming, saith the Lord. You have spiritual discernment through My Holy Spirit, saith the Lord. My children, ask for the gift of discernment as you move forward in Me. Ask for spiritual discernment, saith the Lord."

~ **Discern** what is good or evil. Be sensitive to the Spirit and in the Spirit realm.

~ **Discernment** gives you insight to judge well, not to get tricked by the enemy or to be deceived.

~ **Discernment** gives you spiritual guidance to know right and wrong.

~ **Discernment** through the Holy Spirit is powerful!

Psalm 119 : 125 (NIV) - *''I am your servant; give me discernment that I may understand your statutes.''*

Psalm 119 : 66 (AMP) - *''Teach me good judgment (discernment) and knowledge, For I have believed and trusted and relied on Your commandments.''*

NOTES

What revelation did you receive from this BAM?

_____
_____
_____
_____

Do you have spiritual discernment? Have you ever asked God for the gift of discernment? What areas in your life need discernment?

_____
_____
_____
_____

Be open and honest with God about your current level of discernment. Use this time to write a prayer, asking God for an increase in your ability to discern.

_____
_____
_____
_____

NOTES

THE POWER OF REJECTION

(Has God's Protection)

"I AM in the midst of everything you have prayed for. I AM with you. You are My children. You are the very ones I love so dearly. I must reveal to you the power of rejection. You have the power within you to reject; to reject all the things the devil tries to bring on you. My children, your rejection comes with My Protection; you must reject the devil in your life. You must come against the devil's plan over you. I AM calling for My children to know the power of rejection. I AM calling for My children to reject the plots and schemes of the devil. No longer be intimidated by him. You have the power of rejection to stand against him. My children, reject the devil! DO NOT accept anything from him. You have the power to reject his plans against you. My children, I have given you My Word, My Power, the authority to reject your enemy. You have My full permission to stop the devil from moving in your life. No longer tolerate the least of him and reject the power that I have given you. You have the power and authority to reject the enemy. Use your power through My Word and through My Spirit. Your power of rejection has My Power of Protection, saith the Lord."

JJ: *It took me a minute to understand what God was saying about rejection. So many times in our life, the word rejection meant that someone turned their back on us and did not accept us for who we were. So, imagine my surprise when God was saying that we had the power of rejection and our rejection came with His Protection, but this rejection was slightly different. The rejection that God was speaking of on this day was our power of rejection. The power to reject every assignment, every plot and every scheme that the devil tried to put on God's children. This was something new. It was a new understanding for me. The power of rejection. God's Power that lives in us can come up against anything the devil tries to bring on us. We do not have to accept it. We do not have to accept the devil's mess any longer. We can reject it and not accept it in Jesus' name.*

James 4:7 (NIV) - *"Submit yourself, then, to God. Resist the devil, and he will flee from you."*

James 4:7 (MSG) - *"So, let God work his will in you. Yell a loud No to the devil and watch him make himself scarce."*

Luke 10 : 19 (ESV) - *"Behold, I have given you authority to tread on serpents and scorpions, and over all the power of the enemy, and nothing shall hurt you"*

NOTES

What revelation did you receive from this BAM?

_____
_____
_____
_____
_____

Did you know you have the power to reject the enemy? How can you reject the enemy from operating in your life?

_____
_____
_____
_____
_____

Name the things you are no longer accepting from the enemy.

_____
_____
_____
_____
_____

NOTES

DON'T BE SURPRISED

(Don't Be Surprised With What You See In This World)

"Tell My children that I am coming. Tell My children to get ready for what's to come. Be not surprised when you see the light become dark, when hidden secrets are revealed. Be not distracted by what you see, but move in My Spirit. Remain focused on Me. Do not be afraid of what you will see in this world, saith the Lord. Remain in Me and you will be like a flower that blooms on dry ground, saith the Lord. My children, the time has come when I will pour out My Spirit upon you. I will exalt the ones who exalt Me. I will exalt those who move with humility. I will bless you to be a blessing to others. I will teach you to teach others, saith the Lord.

My children, do not be overwhelmed with the spiritual famine of this world. There are so many ways that spiritual famine can happen, but the greatest spiritual famine is not receiving My Word, saith the Lord.

Remain in Me. Remain in My Word and you will see. You will see more of My Blessings and a greater anointing upon your lives. In the midst of the famine, you will see the love and care that I will pour upon you; for the time has come when the light in you will become brighter and the world will become darker. See to it that you are not surprised when the enemy comes for you. Remain in Me, knowing that he can not touch you, saith the Lord. Do not be moved."

JJ's VISION: *God showed me a beautiful flower blooming on dry, cracked ground. In the center of the desert, the flower was blooming.*

Amos 8 : 11 - 12 (ERV) *- ''The Lord GOD says, "Look, the days are coming when I will cause a famine in the land. The people will not be hungry for bread. They will not be thirsty for water. No, they will be hungry for words from the LORD. The people will wander around the country, from the Dead Sea to the Mediterranean Sea, and from the north part of the country to the east. They will go back and forth looking for a message from the LORD, but they will not find it.''*

John 8 : 12 (NIV) *- ''When Jesus spoke again to the people, he said, "I am the light of the world. Whoever follows me will never walk in darkness, but will have the light of life."*

2 Timothy 3 : 1 (ESV) *- ''But understand this, that in the last days there will come times of difficulty.''*

NOTES

What revelation did you receive from this BAM?

_____
_____
_____
_____

The world is becoming darker. What can you do to make sure God's light remains in you? How can you make sure your light shines brighter?

_____
_____
_____
_____

Have you noticed signs of a spiritual famine in this world? How can you not allow fear to overtake you in the midst of a spiritual famine?

_____
_____
_____
_____

NOTES

STRUGGLES

(Release All Struggles To God)

"My children, no more struggles. Hand them over. Hand them over to Me. No longer carry struggles as you move into your purpose. Do not allow the words, 'I am struggling' to be a part of your vocabulary any longer. My children, when you say that you are struggling, you are saying that you are losing the fight. My children, never allow struggles to become an excuse in your life. Release them to Me. Give them to Me. No longer wear 'I am struggling' as a badge of honor and an excuse to live in situations that were never created for you. My children, never allow the struggles of this world to be a battle within yourself. Struggle is an enemy. Release it to Me. Release everything you have struggled with to Me, saith the Lord. For when you struggle with yourself, you struggle against My Word. My children, never find yourself struggling against My Word, saith the Lord."

Struggle - Conflict, Fight, Strife, Discord, A lack of agreement or harmony, Tussle, War, Battle, A breach of peace

John 16 : 33 (AMP) - *"I have told you these things, so that in Me you may have [perfect] peace. In the world you have tribulation and distress and suffering, but be courageous [be confident, be undaunted, be filled with joy]; I have overcome the world. [My conquest is accomplished, My victory abiding.]"*

Proverbs 18 : 21 (ESV) - *"Death and life are in the power of the tongue, and those who love it will eat its fruits."*

NOTES

What revelation did you receive from this BAM?

_____
_____
_____
_____
_____

Did your perspective on the mindset of 'I am struggling' change after reading this BAM?

_____
_____
_____
_____
_____

How can you release all struggles to God?

_____
_____
_____
_____
_____

NOTES

BECOME SKILLFUL

(Preparation In God's Presence)

"My children, I am calling you into My Presence to prepare you for the revival of souls, to prepare you for the works I have for you to do. My children, there is no greater way to prepare yourself than in My Presence. I AM here. My Presence is here. Come. Come get into My Presence, so that your skills are sharpened, your weapons are confirmed, and your abilities are enhanced. My children, preparation is important to have in these last days, for what I put in you must be refined, sharpened. My children, your skills, gifts and talents are all sharpened in My Presence. Your true development comes through My Word. My Word fully equips you, and being in My Presence makes it official. Being in My Presence makes you official. You have officially been sharpened, saith the Lord."

Official - Authorized, Someone who holds a position of authority

Refine - To bring to a pure state

Sharpen - To become better, To improve, To become sharp, To become skillful

Proverbs 2 : 6 (AMPC) *- "For the Lord gives skillful and godly Wisdom; from His mouth come knowledge and understanding."*

2 Timothy 3 : 16 - 17 (NIV) *- "All Scripture is God-breathed and is useful for teaching, rebuking, correcting and training in righteousness, so that the servant of God may be thoroughly equipped for every good work."*

2 Timothy 3 : 17 (MSG) *- "Through the Word we are put together and shaped up for the tasks God has for us."*

NOTES

What revelation did you receive from this BAM?

_____
_____
_____
_____

Have you been feeling led to get into the Lord's Presence? How is God calling you into His Presence?

_____
_____
_____
_____

Since sharpening your skills requires you to be in the presence of the Lord, how much time are you willing to give God to prepare you for the revival of souls?

_____
_____
_____
_____

NOTES

PICK A TEAM

(What Team Will You Choose?)

''My children are caught in the middle of choosing their team, pulling back and forth from what I have for them to go back to what they are used to. Pick a team; the team you pick will determine your winning season. Pick a team. There is no time to go back and forth wobbling in defeat. Pick My team, saith the Lord.

My children, I AM your winning team. Pick My team. There is no time to waste. You must choose what you want in your life. You must choose what you want for your life. You must stand for what you want, saith the Lord.

The head coach has given you the playbook. It is right in front of you. The playbook is My Word. Pick My team. My team cannot be defeated. My team is The Winning Team. Pick My team, saith the Lord.

My children, how many times do I have to say go? How many times should I tell you that it is your winning season? How many times do I have to tell you, this is the time, and the time is now to move in your faith? My children, you are wasting time in addictions and habits in self-pity, doubt, fear and anxiety. You are pulling away from The Winning Team. Pick a team. Pick The Winning Team, saith the Lord.''

JJ's VISION: *God then showed me a vision of Pulling vs Pushing. There are people, places and things that will pull from you or push you further in your faith. We must choose who we will serve: The Winning Team or the losing team. Pick a team.*

Joshua 24 : 15 (AMP) *- "But as for me and my house, we will serve the Lord."*

Matthew 6 : 24 (ESV) *- "No one can serve two masters, for either he will hate the one and love the other, or he will be devoted to the one and despise the other. You cannot serve God and money."*

1 Corinthians 10 : 21 (ESV) *- "You cannot drink the cup of the Lord and the cup of demons. You cannot partake of the table of the Lord and the table of demons."*

NOTES

What revelation did you receive from this BAM?

_____
_____
_____
_____

What team are you on? How do you know that you are on the right team?

_____
_____
_____
_____

What does it mean to pick God's team; to pick The Winning Team?

_____
_____
_____
_____
_____

NOTES

REMEMBRANCE

(Remember That God Is There For You)

"My children, do you remember the last time I brought you through something? Do you remember the time you felt lost and found at the same time? Do you remember the smallest breakthrough you had? Do you remember the tears you cried, the sadness you felt when someone betrayed you? Do you remember the jokes you told and no one laughed? Do you remember the time you ran out of gas? Do you remember when you were much younger? Do you remember, just yesterday, wondering how you were going to make it? Do you remember crying in pain for someone you have lost? Do you remember the pimple that you felt the whole world could see? Do you remember when your shoes were too tight on your feet? Do you remember when you were scared to sleep in the dark as a child? Do you remember Me? Do you remember My Word from yesterday that could help you today? Do you remember My children? In life, you remember the things that are less important today, but what is important to know is that everything you remember was everything you could not forget. My children, remembrance is a great key when you remember who I AM in your life. What you remember of Me is what I desire for you not to forget, because the smallest of your remembrance is the greatest of My Presence. I have been there all the time, saith the Lord. Go back and remember this with Me. I was there.

Remember what I AM saying to you this day. I AM with you in every way. No matter what people may say to you, I AM with you today and I was with you yesterday. Remember who I AM in your life. It will be important. Remember that I AM with you every day. I AM the One who will make a way for you. My children, remember your faith. Remember My Grace. Remember to pray. Remember to praise. Remember to praise Me. Remember your praise, saith the Lord. Remember Me."

NOTES

What revelation did you receive from this BAM?

_____
_____
_____
_____

Can you remember a time when God was there for you? Describe that moment, whether big or small.

_____
_____
_____
_____

How does it feel knowing that God has been with you in every moment of everyday?

_____
_____
_____
_____

NOTES

BOLDNESS

(Boldness In God)

"Boldness is required in these last days, saith the Lord. You must be bold in Me. Some of My children do not think that they can be bold and humble at the same time. My children, there is boldness in humility, boldness in trusting Me. You can be bold in Me, saith the Lord. Boldness edifies courage and courage edifies confidence, saith the Lord. Your boldness shows that you are confident in Me. Your boldness, courage, humility is what you need, saith the Lord. Be bold in Me."

Boldness - Confidence

Courage - Willing to face things head on, Bravery, Fearless

Edifies - To elevate, To improve, Uplift

---

2 Timothy 1 : 7 (CEB) - "God didn't give us a spirit that is timid but one that is powerful, loving, and self-controlled."

2 Timothy 1 : 7 (AMP) - *"For God did not give us a spirit of timidity or cowardice or fear, but [He has given us a spirit] of power and of love and of sound judgment and personal discipline [abilities that result in a calm, well-balanced mind and self-control]."*

2 Timothy 1 : 7 (ERV) - *"The Spirit God gave us does not make us afraid. His Spirit is a source of power and love and self-control."*

Proverbs 28 : 1 (ERV) - *"The wicked are afraid of everything, but those who live right are as brave as lions."*

NOTES

What revelation did you receive from this BAM?

_____
_____
_____
_____

Did you consider yourself bold before giving your life to Christ? How can you be bold in God?

_____
_____
_____
_____

What does having boldness and confidence in God look like?

_____
_____
_____
_____

NOTES

WEEPING

(God's Children Are Weeping Over The Wrong Things)

"My children are weeping over things that do not matter in My Kingdom, saith the Lord. They are weeping over time and money. They are weeping over material things. They are not concerned about My Kingdom. They are focusing on self, saith the Lord. Their focus is not on building My Kingdom but weeping for self. My children, the life I give you is greater than yourself. It is a life that can be shared with others, a life that can lead others into My Kingdom, but you are weeping over the wrong things that will not inherit My Kingdom. You are crying over dead things and dead situations; crying over spilled milk and not lost souls. My children, stop weeping, saith the Lord and make Me your priority. Make My Word your priority. Make building My Kingdom your priority. Make telling this world about Me your priority. Tell the world about My saving Grace, for I weep over the souls that are lost, saith the Lord."

Philippians 2 : 4 (ESV) - *"Let each of you look not only to his own interests, but also to the interests of others."*

Luke 9 : 23 - 24 (ERV) - *"Jesus continued to say to all of them, "Any of you who want to be my follower must stop thinking about yourself and what you want. You must be willing to carry the cross that is given to you every day for following me. Any of you who try to save the life you have will lose it. But you who give up your life for me will save it."*

Matthew 28 : 18 - 20 (ERV) - *"So he came to them and said, "All authority in heaven and on earth is given to me. So go and make followers of all people in the world. Baptize them in the name of the Father and the Son and the Holy Spirit. Teach them to obey everything that I have told you to do. You can be sure that I will be with you always. I will continue with you until the end of time."*

NOTES

What revelation did you receive from this BAM?

_____
_____
_____
_____

Are there dead situations that you are weeping over?

_____
_____
_____
_____

How can you make building the Kingdom of God your priority?

_____
_____
_____
_____

NOTES

SCOFFER

(Don't Worry About The Scoffers)

"My children, in the midst of your scoffers, I AM with you, saith the Lord. Scoffers are hecklers. Do not be moved by hecklers, for I AM with you. My children, scoffers are there to cause you to doubt yourself and hecklers are there to distract your attention. Do not be moved by what they say or do, for I AM with you, saith the Lord. This is a word for My people.

My children, where I am sending you, the scoffers become greater and the hecklers become louder. Refuse their sounds and follow Me. Follow Me. Close your ears to the sound of the enemy and hear only My Voice. Hear Me. Hear what I have spoken to you and believe what I will show you, saith the Lord. Stand firm in Me. Listen to My Voice and I will protect you, saith the Lord. Hear Me; only hear My Voice, for the closer you get to Me, the louder your enemy will be, saith the Lord."

Scoffer - Someone who laughs and speaks about a person or idea in a way that shows that they think that person or idea is stupid or silly, Mocker

Heckler - There to interrupt you by being loud, making rude ugly remarks, laughing and shouting criticisms and insults, Troublemaker

Mocker of God - Someone who defies and renounces the truth of God, not only to their own detriment but to the destruction of others.

2 Peter 3 : 3 (ESV) - *"Knowing this first of all, that scoffers will come in the last days with scoffing, following their own sinful desires."*

Proverbs 21 : 24 (ESV) - *" 'Scoffer' is the name of the arrogant, haughty man who acts with arrogant pride."*

Psalm 35 : 1 (TPT) - *"O Lord, fight for me! Harass the hecklers: accuse my accusers. Fight those who fight against me."*

Psalm 35 : 1 - 3 (MSG) - *"Harass these hecklers, GOD, punch these bullies in the nose. Grab a weapon, anything at hand; stand up for me! Get ready to throw the spear, aim the javelin, at the people who are out to get me. Reassure me; let me hear you say, 'I'll save you.'"*

NOTES

What revelation did you receive from this BAM?

_____
_____
_____
_____
_____

Did your perspective on scoffers and hecklers change after reading this BAM?

_____
_____
_____
_____
_____

How can you continue to move forward into what God has called for you to do, despite the actions of scoffers, hecklers or the enemy?

_____
_____
_____
_____
_____

NOTES

RELY ON GOD

(God Is Your Source)

"My children, you must trust and rely on Me. Do not allow anything to come before Me, saith the Lord. I will not be outsourced, for I AM your source. You must rely on Me, saith the Lord. I will provide for your every need, for I AM the source of all good things; the only source that you need, saith the Lord. Do not make anything your source. Do not place others as your source. I AM your only source. Do not allow anything to come before Me. Do not outsource Me; for I will not be outsourced. I AM your source, saith the Lord."

Source - Origin, The point or place where something begins, From which something comes or can be obtained

Outsource - Going outside of the internal source

Jehovah Jireh - God is your provider

Genesis 22 : 14 (AMP) - "So Abraham named that place, The LORD Will Provide. And it is said to this day, "On the mountain of the LORD it will be seen and provided."

Philippians 4 : 19 - 20 (AMP) - *"And my God will liberally supply (fill until full) your every need according to His riches in glory in Christ Jesus. To our God and Father be the glory forever and ever. Amen."*

Exodus 34 : 14 (ESV) - *"for you shall worship no other god, for the LORD, whose name is Jealous, is a jealous God,"*

Psalm 23 : 1 (NIV) - *"The LORD is my shepherd, I lack nothing."*

1 Corinthians 8 : 6 (AMPC) - *"Yet for us there is [only] one God, the Father, Who is the Source of all things "*

NOTES

What revelation did you receive from this BAM?

_____
_____
_____
_____
_____

How have you been relying on God as your source? How can you rely on God even more?

_____
_____
_____
_____
_____

How can you make sure to put nothing before God? How can you make sure that God is your only source?

_____
_____
_____
_____
_____

NOTES

WHEN YOU ARE WEAK, I AM STRONG
(Your Strength Comes From God)

"I want My children to know that they can find their strength in Me. There are areas in your life that you are pondering on your weakness, saith the Lord. But when you are weak, I AM strong. I will cover you and strengthen you, saith the Lord. My children, when you are weak, come to Me for strength. No longer allow 'I am weak' to be an excuse, saith the Lord. Your strength will always come from Me. Grab a hold of your strength in Me, for weakness in the flesh is a trap from the enemy. Be strong in Me, for your strength will always come from Me. Your strength will come through My Word and through your faith and your belief.

My children, your strength will come from Me."

Isaiah 41 : 10 (ESV) - *"Fear not, for I am with you; be not dismayed, for I am your God; I will strengthen you, I will help you, I will uphold you with my righteous right hand."*

Philippians 4 : 13 (ESV) - *"I can do all things through Him who strengthens me."*

Ephesians 6 : 10 (ESV) - *"Finally, be strong in the Lord and in the strength of his might."*

1 Chronicles 16 : 11 (ESV) - *"Seek the LORD and his strength; seek his presence continually!"*

Exodus 15 : 2 (ESV) - *"The LORD is my strength and my song, and he has become my salvation; this is my God, and I will praise him, my father's God, and I will exalt him."*

Isaiah 40 : 31 (ESV) - *"but they who wait for the LORD shall renew their strength; they shall mount up with wings like eagles; they shall run and not be weary; they shall walk and not faint."*

NOTES

What revelation did you receive from this BAM?

_____
_____
_____
_____
_____

How can you lay hold of God's strength?

_____
_____
_____
_____
_____

Describe a time when God showed you He was the source of your strength.

_____
_____
_____
_____
_____

NOTES

IT IS IN YOU

(God's Power Is In Us)

"My power is within you. My Holy Spirit is within you. My children, you cannot fight the devil without My Word and My Power. My children, My Power and Authority is the greatest thing that you can have and one of the greatest things that I have given you, saith the Lord. My Power moves mountains, heals the sick, casts out demons and releases My Promises over your life, saith the Lord.

The world's power, self-power, cannot compare to My Power: My Holy Spirit that is within you. My children, the evil powers of this world make a man think that he has the power, but it is My Power that has the authority to stop this world and to remove evil from it, saith the Lord.

My Power causes the enemy to fall at My Feet and obey Me. My children, there is nothing to be afraid of when you have My Word, My Power, My Holy Spirit within you. What can man do to you? Who shall you fear or what shall you fear? This is the same power that raised Lazarus from the dead. The same power that heals the sick, restores the brokenhearted and releases miracles in your life. The same power that the devil is afraid of. The same power that he does not want you to know you have in Me.

My children, the enemy knows My Power and sees My Power. When you know My Power, you will know your power, saith the Lord. My Power is in you. My Spirit is within you; your power is in Me. Do not be afraid to stand in the power that I have given you, the power to subdue. Do not fear the one who fears the power in you. Stay in My Presence and live in My Presence, for being in My Presence will cause My Power to be revealed in you, saith the Lord."

---

2 Timothy 1 : 7 (ESV) - *"for God gave us a spirit not of fear but of power and love and self-control."*

Luke 10 : 19 (ESV) - *"Behold, I have given you authority to tread on serpents and scorpions, and over all the power of the enemy, and nothing shall hurt you."*

Psalm 62 : 11 (NIV) - *"Once God has spoken; twice have I heard this: that power belongs to God,"*

Acts 1 : 8 (ESV) - *"But you will receive power when the Holy Spirit has come upon you, and you will be my witnesses in Jerusalem and in all Judea and Samaria, and to the end of the earth."*

NOTES

What revelation did you receive from this BAM?

_____
_____
_____
_____

Did your perspective on God's power change after reading this BAM? How can you receive a deeper understanding of God's power within you?

_____
_____
_____
_____
_____

Describe a time in the Bible where God displayed His Mighty Power. How can this story relate to you?

_____
_____
_____
_____
_____

NOTES

FIREPLACE

(A Fire Within Us)

"My children, seek that place within you that will cause My Fire to burn. Be aware of the fire within you. It represents My Presence, My Power, My Spirit, My Love, My Everlasting Flame, saith the Lord. I am teaching you about the very part of Me that should always burn within you. It is that desire to want more of Me. It is a fire that lives in every part of your life. It is what I have waited so long for you to have. My Fire, saith the Lord.

My children, I want you to understand My Fire. It is My Spirit, My Anointing that cannot be contained. It is a continual fire that burns within you. It is a fire that goes deep into your spirit man and dwells in a place that only I can enter. It is a place that few of My children know of. This Fire will cause you to draw closer to Me, saith the Lord. My children, it is time for you to draw closer to Me, to seek My Fire, to seek a deeper relationship with Me, to seek a deeper anointing in your life, saith the Lord.

My children, the fire of My anointing, My Spirit is waiting to burn inside of you. Completely surrender your all to Me and learn about My Fire, My Holy Spirit, saith the Lord, and you will learn more about Me. Stand in My Fire and you will not burn. For it is a sacred place that you will reach when you are in My Presence.

Hebrews 12 : 29 (ESV) - *"For our God is a consuming fire."*

Hebrews 12 : 28 - 29 (MSG) - *"Do you see what we've got? An unshakable kingdom! And do you see how thankful we must be? Not only thankful, but brimming with worship, deeply reverent before God. For God is not an indifferent bystander. He's actively cleaning house, torching all that needs to burn, and he won't quit until it's all cleansed. God himself is Fire!"*

NOTES

What revelation did you receive from this BAM?

_____
_____
_____
_____
_____

Have you ever felt the Fire of God?

_____
_____
_____
_____

How can you seek the Lord on a deeper level? How can you seek the place where the Lord's fire burns within you?

_____
_____
_____
_____
_____

NOTES

REBUILD

(Rebuild Your Relationship With God)

"My children, it is time to rebuild your relationship with Me, saith the Lord. Rebuild what has been broken. My children, the time has come that your spirit must be right with Me. I AM coming soon, saith the Lord and you must rebuild. Rebuild your relationship with Me by choosing Me, saith the Lord. There is so much going on in this world and I am calling for My children to rebuild the closeness that you had with Me. The time has come for you to choose life or death. I will no longer accept half of you. I am calling for all of you to be complete and whole in Me.

My children, rebuild in Me. Build My Spirit stronger in you than it has ever been. Your strength and courage to rebuild your relationship with Me will cause My Spirit to fall down on you. There is no time to waste. You must choose to keep our relationship strong and to defend your choice to choose Me, to choose My Love, to choose life until I come, saith the Lord. I am calling for My children to build their relationship stronger in Me. Things are going to happen on this earth and if your relationship is not strong in Me, you will fall and be deceived. For if you are not choosing Me, you are not choosing life with Me, and without My Word and your love for Me, you will fall and be deceived, saith the Lord."

Joshua 24 : 14 - 15 (ESV) - *"Now therefore fear the LORD and serve him in sincerity and in faithfulness. Put away the gods that your fathers served beyond the River and in Egypt, and serve the LORD. And if it is evil in your eyes to serve the LORD, choose this day whom you will serve, whether the gods your fathers served in the region beyond the River, or the gods of the Amorites in whose land you dwell. But as for me and my house, we will serve the LORD."*

JJ takes it to the streets: *Your decision to serve God, to rebuild or to build your relationship with God is important. You can no longer play with God with your decision. You have to choose this day whom you will serve. You're either going to be cold or hot. There is no lukewarm in God. You are either black or white. There are no gray areas serving God. God is serious about your relationship with Him, so get serious about rebuilding your relationship with Him, before it is too late.*

NOTES

What revelation did you receive from this BAM?

_____
_____
_____
_____
_____

Describe your relationship with God.

_____
_____
_____
_____
_____

How can you build a stronger relationship with God?

_____
_____
_____
_____
_____

NOTES

PREPARATION | WARNING

(A Storm Is Coming For This World)

"My children, a storm is coming for this world. This storm does not belong to you. It is not for you, saith the Lord. Stay focused on Me, for you will see a storm on one side of this world and sunshine on the other. The sunshine is for you. You will see blessings on one side and disasters on another; the blessings are for you. You will see famine on one side and a harvest on another; the harvest is for you. Do not fret in the midst of this storm and in the midst of the shaking; no harm will come to you. Remain in Me, saith the Lord.

My children, in this storm, your trust in Me will be your anchor. Your faith will be your shield. This world will shake and those that are of this world will shake too. But do not be afraid, for I will cover you. I will protect you. I will bless you even in the midst of the storm, saith the Lord. My children, in the midst of the shaking and in the midst of the storm, blessings will be upon My children: blessings upon the ones who serve Me and blessings upon the ones who put their faith and trust in Me; they will be your anchor, saith the Lord."

JJ's VISION: *God gave me a vision of a storm on my right side and a beautiful calm field on the left side. There was a line drawn down the middle that separated the two. This was a warning from God. He has drawn the line.*

Proverbs 10 : 25 (NIV) *- "When the storm has swept by, the wicked are gone, but the righteous stand firm forever."*

Job 5 : 20 - 21 (GNT) *- "when famine comes, he will keep you alive, and in war protect you from death. God will rescue you from slander; he will save you when destruction comes."*

NOTES

What revelation did you receive from this BAM?

_____
_____
_____
_____
_____

How can you focus on God in the midst of the storm coming to this world? How can you remain on the side of blessings and harvest?

_____
_____
_____
_____
_____

Have you noticed a beginning to this storm? Is the storm already here? What signs have you noticed about this coming storm?

_____
_____
_____
_____

NOTES

RELIABLE
(Are You Reliable?)

"My children, are you reliable? Can I rely on you? This is the time to answer that question. Answer it honestly. Can I rely on you to be My chosen one? Can I trust you to do what you say you will do? Can I rely on you? Can I trust you? Are you reliable? Are you trustworthy to receive the blessings that are falling? Can I trust you to trust Me? Can I trust you to give at a moment's notice?

My children, reliability and consistency are a part of Me, for I AM consistent. I AM reliable. I AM trustworthy and I AM constant. Know this day how important it is for you to be reliable, dependable and consistent in serving Me. Know how important it is for you to do what you say you will do and go where you say you will go. Let the words that come out of your mouth be words that are trustworthy, reliable, dependable and never changing, saith the Lord. My children, a reliable trustworthy child of God, represents a reliable trustworthy God. Are you reliable? Can I trust you, saith the Lord?"

Ecclesiastes 5 : 4 - 5 (NIV) - "When you make a vow to God, do not delay to fulfill it. He has no pleasure in fools; fulfill your vow. It is better not to make a vow than to make one and not fulfill it."

NOTES

What revelation did you receive from this BAM?

_____
_____
_____
_____
_____

Are you reliable? Can God rely on you? Answer this question honestly.

_____
_____
_____
_____
_____

What can you do to show God that you are trustworthy and reliable?

_____
_____
_____
_____
_____

NOTES

SERVE ME FIRST
(I AM First)

"My children, understand this, when I AM not first in your life, your life is out of order. My children, you are putting Me last, in the middle and even at the end in your life. You have not made Me your priority, saith the Lord. You are putting the ways of this world before Me, by serving others before you are serving Me. You are putting your family, spouses, kids, career, friends, people and things before Me, saith the Lord. My children, I come first! I come first in your life. I come before everything and everyone. I AM a first place God, not fit for second place. Everything starts with Me and everything ends with Me, saith the Lord. I AM Alpha and Omega, The Beginning and The End, The First and The Last. Nothing comes before Me, and nothing will come after Me. You must know to put Me first in your life. When you make Me a priority, your life will be in order, saith the Lord."

Matthew 6 : 33 (ESV) - *"But seek first the kingdom of God and his righteousness, and all these things will be added to you."*

1 Samuel 12 : 24 (ESV) - *"Only fear the L*ORD *and serve him faithfully with all your heart. For consider what great things he has done for you."*

Colossians 3 : 23 - 24 (NKJV) - *"And whatever you do, do it heartily, as to the Lord and not to men, knowing that from the Lord you will receive the reward of the inheritance; for you serve the Lord Christ."*

Deuteronomy 6 : 5 (ESV) - *"You shall love the LORD your God with all your heart and with all your soul and with all your might."*

1 Chronicles 16 : 11 (ESV) - *"Seek the LORD and his strength; seek his presence continually!"*

NOTES

What revelation did you receive from this BAM?

_____
_____
_____
_____

Did you know that God comes before everyone and everything in your life? Are there any areas in your life where you have neglected God as your priority? Name these areas.

_____
_____
_____
_____
_____

How can you serve God first in your life? How can you make Him your priority?

_____
_____
_____
_____
_____

NOTES

MY THOUGHTS

(What God Thinks About You)

"If you only knew how I really feel about you, you will know that My Love for you is everlasting. I desire so much for you; I desire for you to see yourself as I see you. My children, My Love for you carries you when you are hurting and disappointed. It cares about every tear that falls from your eyes. My Love for you cries. I cry. Every part of Me Loves you. Every part of Me seeks to be with you. I Love you for everlasting. I Love you for eternity. Do not doubt My Love, for everyday when you wake up, look around and you will see; you will see My Love. Look not in the evil, disheartening, crushing spirit of this world, but look at the beauty in My Love. There is beauty in when you take your first breath, beauty in the sound when you call on My Name, beauty that is in you when you are trying to understand who I AM in your life, beauty when you seek Me, beauty when you truly desire My Will. It is beautiful.

My children, My Thoughts of you are precious, for you are unique in every way. You are the apple of My Eye; you're wonderfully made. You are in My Heart and My Spirit is in you. You are the fruit of My Love, the Love that I have for you. My children, My Thoughts are thoughts of you. If you only knew, only knew how much I Love you, you will rest in Me, rest in My Love, rest safely, saith the Lord. My children, when I think of you, I can't help but to smile. It is the Love in My Heart for My child. My children, there is no greater Love for you to have, no greater Love for you to know, no greater Love to feel, than the Love that I show you.

I Love you, saith the Lord.''

John 3 : 16 (NIV) - *''For God so loved the world that he gave his one and only Son, that whoever believes in him shall not perish but have eternal life.''*

I John 4 : 19 (NIV) - *''We love because He first loved us''*

1 John 4 : 16 (NIV) - *''And so we know and rely on the love God has for us. God is love. Whoever lives in love lives in God, and God in them.''*

Psalms 136 : 26 (NIV) - *''Give Thanks to the Lord, for He is good. His love endures forever.''*

NOTES

What revelation did you receive from this BAM?

_____
_____
_____
_____
_____

How does it feel to know that God has His Mind on you? How does it feel to know the way God thinks of you? In what ways do you think of Him?

_____
_____
_____
_____
_____

Describe a time when God showed you His Love.

_____
_____
_____
_____
_____

NOTES

BREAKTHROUGH

(Spiritual Revival)

"Your breakthroughs start within you and through you, saith the Lord. Your breaking point is here. A Revival within you. My children, break away from everything that has caused you distractions in your life, spiritual hindrance that caused you not to grow in Me. Your personal revival is here. Your season is open to receive and retrieve what is yours. You are at your breaking point. Break away from the things that stop you from moving in Me. Breaking point, where you are no longer allowing yourself to remain in bondage, but to be set free, saith the Lord. This is your breakthrough season, a revival that starts within you. My children, stay focused on Me. Do not look to the left or the right. Do not be distracted by what you have broken free from. Keep going, straight ahead. Look forward not backwards, saith the Lord. My Revival starts within you."

Proverbs 4 : 25 - 27 (AMP) - *"Let your eyes look directly ahead and let your gaze be fixed straight in front of you. Consider well and watch carefully the path of your feet and all your ways will be steadfast and sure. Do not turn away to the right nor the left; turn your foot from evil."*

NOTES

What revelation did you receive from this BAM?

_____
_____
_____
_____
_____

How can you block distractions? How can you make sure to look straight ahead, not to the left or right?

_____
_____
_____
_____
_____

What things can you break away from to stay focused on the Lord?

_____
_____
_____
_____
_____

NOTES

OUTBURST

(Sudden Blessings)

"My children, the time for the sudden outburst of My Blessings is here, saith the Lord. Listen clearly to understand. Within your suddenly, there will be an outburst of My Blessings, outburst of My Favor. My children, what you are believing that I will do, believe bigger. Do not limit your belief in a season of suddenly. This is the time for sudden outbursts. My outburst will flow through other countries. It will flow through nations, it will flow through you. My children, My Thoughts are higher than your thoughts, but I am calling for your thoughts to go bigger, bigger to release Me to go grander in your life. No longer think small. You cannot imagine what I have for you. No longer think small. I am ready to show up in the outburst. I am releasing the sudden outburst in your life. Heaven's Gates are open. You can no longer think small. Your faith will cause the sudden outburst, for I am doing a new thing, a greater thing in you. Heaven's Gates are open now, so release Me from the small box, the small box you put Me in. Your faith and believing big will allow Me to show out in your life.

My children, going big has caused fear in your life. Big was intimidating for My children, but you serve a big God. I AM a big God. Everything I have done was always done big. My children, do not limit yourself and do not limit Me. It is time to show this world who I AM and who you are in Me, saith the Lord."

Outburst - Sudden release, Outpouring

Isaiah 55 : 8 (MSG) - *"I don't think the way you think. The way you work isn't the way I work. God's decree. For as the sky soars high above earth, so the way I work surpasses the way you work, and the way I think is beyond the way you think."*

Ephesians 3 : 20 (KJV) - *"Now unto him that is able to do exceedingly abundantly above all that we ask or think, according to the power that worketh in us."*

NOTES

What revelation did you receive from this BAM?

_____
_____
_____
_____
_____

Has anything limited your way of thinking? What can you do to think bigger? How can you come out of small thinking and walk into bigger faith?

_____
_____
_____
_____
_____

What dreams and goals do you have? Believe even bigger than that.

_____
_____
_____
_____
_____

NOTES

MORE VALUABLE THAN MONEY

(The Principles of God)

"My children, ask yourself, 'The God who has everything and all things, is He not more valuable than money?' Money has been a spirit that has controlled My children because they did not understand money. Don't get Me wrong, My children, in this world, money is something to have, but you cannot allow money to have you. Some of My children treat money as their god. They worship money and worship the people who have money. You look up to people with money. Money has controlled you because you had no understanding of it. They tell you that money can buy you anything on earth, and some of My children have sold themselves for it. I ask you, if money can buy you anything on this earth, what can your faith do in heaven and on the earth?

I am pouring out My financial blessings on My children and you must understand My principles with money. You must not lose faith when you receive your financial blessings and return to thinking that it is yours. It is to be used to further My Kingdom on earth. You must not worship the money. Do not worship the money you have, for it will disappear. My children, let Me be clear, do not take yourself back to believing that you received these financial blessings on your own, for it is I who pours out blessings on you.

My children, you need My Wisdom, My Stewardship to help guide you through the process of not having the money, to receiving your overflow; for what I put in your hands, belongs to My Kingdom. Don't forget it, saith the Lord. It belongs to Me.''

---

1 Timothy 6 : 9 - 10 (NIV) - *''Those who want to get rich fall into temptation and a trap and into many foolish and harmful desires that plunge people into ruin and destruction. For the love of money is a root of all kinds of evil. Some people, eager for money, have wandered from the faith and pierced themselves with many griefs.''*

Hebrews 13 : 5 - 6 (MSG) - *''Don't be upset with getting more material things. Be relaxed with what you have. Since God assured us, "I'll never let you down, never walk off and leave you" we can boldly quote, "God is there, ready to help; I am fearless no matter what. Who or what can get to me?''*

Ecclesiastes 5 : 10 - 11 (MSG) - *"The one who loves money is never satisfied with money, Nor the one who loves wealth with big profits. More smoke. The more loot you get, the more looters show up. And what fun is that to be robbed in broad daylight?"*

Matthew 6 : 24 (NIV) - *"No one can serve two masters. Either you will hate the one and love the other, or you will be devoted to the one and despise the other. You cannot serve both God and money."*

NOTES

What revelation did you receive from this BAM?

_____
_____
_____
_____
_____

Have you ever felt controlled by money? Did you ever think that faith is greater than money? How can you build your faith in God to not allow money to control you?

_____
_____
_____
_____
_____

God is requiring stewardship over His Blessings. Do you know how to steward the blessings of God? Write down scriptures that talk about God's Stewardship.

_____
_____
_____
_____
_____

NOTES

CLARITY AND DIRECTION

(God Is Leading Us)

"So many of My children are asking for clarity in their lives. Some of you are seeking direction outside of Me, for which way your life should go. I tell you My children, seek Me first and you will get your answer, saith the Lord.

I AM directing you, but you have become impatient in waiting for directions from Me. You have become frustrated in thinking that you do not know which way your life is going, saith the Lord.

My children, every one of My Plans for your life has direction. Be patient. I will direct you to the very things that I have for you. Do not allow worry to confuse your sense of direction. Know that I AM leading you. Get quiet in Me. Seek Me and you will hear Me, and you will see Me. Fill yourself up with joy, knowing that the Lord your God is directing you; for I have a plan for you, and there is clarity in My Plan for your life. I AM directing you and preparing you for where I have for you to go. Get into a quiet place. Shhhhh, for I AM directing your life, saith the Lord."

VISION: *God then showed me a vision of a police officer, standing in the center of the intersection, directing traffic. The police officer was directing traffic by stopping people when it was their time to be stopped. He was allowing people to go when it was their time to go. I noticed while the police officer was directing traffic, there seemed to be nothing but order in the streets. Nothing was chaotic.*

We must allow God to be the center of our lives, directing us in the way that we should go. If we don't allow God to direct us, we can cause a traffic jam, full of worry, stress and frustration. When this happens, it can cloud your true sense of direction.

Psalms 37 : 23 - 24 (AMP) - *"The steps of a good and righteous man are directed and established by the Lord, and he delights in his way and blesses his path. When he falls, he will not be hurled down because the Lord is the one who holds his hand and sustains him."*

Proverbs 3 : 5 - 6 (KJV) - *"Trust in the Lord with all thine heart and lean not unto your own understanding. In all your ways acknowledge him, and he shall direct thy paths."*

NOTES

What revelation did you receive from this BAM?

_____
_____
_____
_____

How can you get into a quiet place with God to receive clarity and direction?

_____
_____
_____
_____

How can you trust in the Lord's Will and direction for your life? How can you rest in His guidance?

_____
_____
_____
_____

NOTES

DEFINE YOURSELF IN ME

(Tell your story)

"For too long the devil has held on to your story: your experiences, your tragedies, your mistakes. He has held you captive to them, saith the Lord. He has used some of your life decisions to chain you up; chain you up in your mind with shame and regrets. But I AM here to set the captive free and heal the brokenhearted, saith the Lord. Do not allow the enemy to hold on to your past; do not be defined by your past. Be free in My Presence, saith the Lord. My children, I see your life from the beginning to the end and the devil has held on to your story. For his reasons, he has held you in shame and guilt, worried about what others will think or say about your life. The enemy has held onto your life story; a story that the enemy is afraid for you to tell. Do not allow the enemy to hold you hostage to your life story. Tell your story.

It is time to release your book, saith the Lord. Be not ashamed My children, for everyone has a story. The question is, who is telling your story? Who are you allowing to define you in your story? Who can edit your story? I AM the only one who can edit your life story to give you a better ending. I AM the only one who can make the experiences in your story your testimony, saith the Lord. My children, do not be afraid to tell your story. Tell about how I brought you through, saith the Lord. My children, you must understand this; an untold story is a book that has never been written. A book that has never been written is a book that could never be read. A book that is never read is a testimony that has never been heard, saith the Lord."

Psalm 107 : 2 (NIV) - *"Let the redeemed of the LORD tell their story— those he redeemed from the hand of the foe,"*

Psalm 119 : 46 (ESV) - *"I will also speak of your testimonies before kings and shall not be put to shame,"*

NOTES

What revelation did you receive from this BAM?

_____
_____
_____
_____
_____

Are you ready to tell your story? What untold story are you no longer ashamed to tell?

_____
_____
_____
_____

Are you ready for your book release? Are you ready for God to get the Glory from your story? What's the title of your story? Begin writing your story now.

_____
_____
_____
_____
_____

NOTES

WRESTLE

(Fighting Against Peace)

"My children, why do you fight against something that is already yours to have? Why do you pray for peace and will not receive it? Why do you make your way hard? You make your way so hard that even you do not understand it. Why do you wrestle against peace? My children, in My Presence, there is peace, saith the Lord. You have caused everything to be at war within you because you will not receive My Peace. The battle is not yours. Stop wrestling and fighting against peace. Peace is yours to receive, saith the Lord. I say to you My children, when you wrestle, when you fight, when you struggle with peace in your life, you are going into a full battle against peace. You're in a boxing ring fighting against PEACE. You must REST My children; rest in My Peace, saith the Lord."

JJ: The word "REST" sits right in the middle of the word "WRESTLE"

When you don't REST, you WRESTLE.

Peace = Rest = Stillness = Quietness

Peace is quiet and it could be too quiet for those of you who are used to the noise in your life. Seek God's Peace. There is rest in Him.

Psalm 4 : 8 (ESV) - *''In peace I will both lie down and sleep; for you alone, O Lord, make me dwell in safety.''*

John 14 : 27 (ESV) - *''Peace I leave with you; my peace I give to you. Not as the world gives do I give to you. Let not your hearts be troubled, neither let them be afraid.''*

Isaiah 26 : 3 (ESV) - *''You keep him in perfect peace whose mind is stayed on you, because he trusts in you.''*

NOTES

What revelation did you receive from this BAM?

_____
_____
_____
_____
_____

Has there ever been a time in your life where you fought against Peace? Describe the time when you were wrestling with Peace.

_____
_____
_____
_____
_____

What is your understanding of rest? How can you rest in God's Presence? How can you rest in His Peace?

_____
_____
_____
_____
_____

NOTES

SET APART

(God Has Set You Apart)

"I have set you apart. I have set you apart, saith the Lord. I have called you to be set apart in this world. My children, the time has come when right will be wrong, and wrong will be right. Do not be afraid to stand up for what is right in My Word. Do not be afraid to stand up through My Spirit. You must remain upright through My Word. You must remain in Me, saith the Lord. For I have called you to be set apart; to live in a way that is pleasing to Me, to stand firmly in the authority that I have given you, to live holy in Me, to live upright through My Spirit, saith the Lord. My children, know this, to be set apart is to be chosen. You have been chosen to live Holy in Me, chosen to live with Me, saith the Lord."

Set Apart = Holy

Leviticus 20 : 26 (ESV) - *"You shall be holy to me, for I the LORD am holy and have separated you from the peoples, that you should be mine."*

1 Peter 1 : 15 - 16 (ESV) - *"But as he who called you is holy, you also be holy in all your conduct, since it is written, 'You shall be holy, for I am holy.'"*

NOTES

What revelation did you receive from this BAM?

_____
_____
_____
_____
_____

What does it mean to be set apart? What does it mean to stand upright in God?

_____
_____
_____
_____
_____

How can you live a life of holiness?

_____
_____
_____
_____
_____

NOTES

OBEDIENCE IS PRICELESS

(The Cost Of Disobedience Is Famine)

''My children, there is a difference between more than enough and not enough. I AM more than enough, saith the Lord. Your obedience calls for Me to be more than enough in your life, saith the Lord. Your disobedience to My Word has caused a famine to be released on this Earth. The time for obedience is here. The time for your obedience is now. My children, your obedience to My Word is attached to My more than enough, My unlimited supply, saith the Lord. Your disobedience is attached to famine, famine that I have released on this earth, saith the Lord.

My children, I AM separating the obedient from the disobedient, the limitless from the limited, the powerful from the powerless, the priceless from the prideful. When you choose obedience, you choose to go higher and deeper in Me. When you choose disobedience, the outcome is famine and destruction, saith the Lord.''

Luke 6 : 46 (NIV) - *"Why do you call me, 'Lord, Lord,' and do not do what I say?"*

Deuteronomy 28 : 1 (ESV) - *''And if you faithfully obey the voice of the* L<small>ORD</small> *your God, being careful to do all his commandments that I command you today, the* L<small>ORD</small> *your God will set you high above all the nations of the earth.*

Deuteronomy 5 : 33 (NIV) - *"Walk in obedience to all that the LORD your God has commanded you, so that you may live and prosper and prolong your days in the land that you will possess."*

Deuteronomy 28 : 15 - 16 (NIV) - *"However, if you do not obey the LORD your God and do not carefully follow all his commands and decrees I am giving you today, all these curses will come on you and overtake you: You will be cursed in the city and cursed in the country."*

1 Samuel 15 : 23 (ERV) - *"Refusing to obey is as bad as the sin of sorcery. Being stubborn and doing what you want is like the sin of worshiping idols. You refused to obey the LORD's command, so he now refuses to accept you as king."*

NOTES

What revelation did you receive from this BAM?

_____
_____
_____
_____
_____

Did you know that disobedience was attached to famine? How can you be sure not to pay the cost of disobedience?

_____
_____
_____
_____
_____

Did you know obedience was attached to God's more than enough? How can you be sure to receive the cost of obedience?

_____
_____
_____
_____
_____

NOTES

PRAY

(Time To Pray)

"My children, the time is now to pray; pray in the morning, pray in the evening, pray when you wake up, pray when you lie down. Pray for your family, pray for your children. Teach your children to pray, pray over your homes every day. Pray for the lost souls that are in this world, pray for every boy and every girl, saith the Lord. Pray for the nations. Pray for your country, pray for your city and state. Pray for the Church, pray for the poor, pray for the weak, pray for the strong. Pray for the refugees. Pray for the foreigners. Pray for the lost souls to return home.

My children, it is time to pray. Pray for My laborers that are in the fields. Pray for the very ones I have sent to do My Will. Pray for the lost that they will be found, pray that the wickedness be revealed. Pray for your enemies. Pray for insight, pray for strength. Pray for miracles, pray for protection. Pray that My Will be done, saith the Lord.

My children, the time is now to pray. Pray, for I AM coming soon. At that time, I will cry, cry for the very ones who did not choose Me, who did not serve Me on this earth; the ones that I can not take home to spend eternity with Me. My children, come and pray. Pray for the lost souls in this world, pray in My Name. Pray with a sincere heart, for the time is now to pray, saith the Lord."

Matthew 6 : 9 - 13 (ESV) - *''This, then, is how you should pray: 'Our Father in heaven, hallowed be your name, your kingdom come, your will be done, on earth as it is in heaven. Give us today our daily bread. And forgive us our debts, as we also have forgiven our debtors. And lead us not into temptation, but deliver us from the evil one.'''*

1 Thessalonians 5 : 17 (ESV) - *''pray without ceasing,''*

NOTES

What revelation did you receive from this BAM?

_____
_____
_____
_____
_____

How often do you pray?

_____
_____
_____
_____
_____

What can you do to pray more? How can you allow God to take you to a deeper level of prayer?

_____
_____
_____
_____
_____

NOTES

PRAYER OF COMMITMENT

I am committed to Jesus Christ. I will honor Christ in my actions and deeds. I will obey God's Word, no matter the pain or cost. I will remain committed to Jesus Christ. Even when it seems hard to do, I will follow Him and I will do what God has called me to do. No matter what, no matter who, I am committed to Christ. I will not let anything or anyone break my commitment to Jesus Christ. I will serve Him with my whole heart. I will pray and give thanks to Him at all times. I will not allow my flesh or thoughts to sin against Him. I am a servant of Christ, and I am here to serve, to serve Him only. I am committed to serve My Lord and Savior Jesus Christ.

Amen

DECREES

WAKE UP DECREE

Good morning, Father. Good morning, Jesus. Good morning, Holy Spirit.

Father God, thank you for waking me up and giving me another day. I surrender my all to you this day. I decree that Your Will be done in my life and in my family's life today, in Jesus name. Lord, I cease the operation of the enemy in our lives today. I stand in my authority, that Jesus has given me, and I bind up all plots and schemes of the enemy, in Jesus name, and loose your warrior angels from heaven to protect me and my family today.

I decree that the Holy Spirit leads me and guides me into truth this day in Jesus name. Amen. (John 16:13)

COMING INTO GOD'S PRESENCE

Father God, forgive me for all my sins and cleanse me from all unrighteousness, in the name of Jesus. I come into Your Presence with thanksgiving. I decree that in Your Presence, there is fullness of joy. I bow before You to worship You, to honor You and to give You praise. I present my body this day, as a living sacrifice, holy and acceptable to you. Lord, have Your Will in my life, in Jesus name. Amen. (Romans 12:1)

BLESSING THE LORD IN HIS PRESENCE

Father God, today I deny myself, my flesh, and my ways, and pick up the cross and follow Jesus. I bless You today with all that is within me. My mind blesses the Lord. My eyes bless the Lord; my hands and feet bless the Lord. Everything that is within me and around me, bow down and bless the Lord.

I surrender my all to You, in Jesus name. Amen.

FORGIVENESS

I understand that when I forgive others, according to Matthew 6:15, God will forgive me. If I do not forgive others, God will not forgive me. I decree that I have a forgiving heart, therefore, I forgive others of their trespasses and God forgives me. I understand that forgiveness is good for my health: spiritually and physically, therefore, I choose to forgive, in Jesus Name. Amen

HEALTH

I decree that God will restore my health and heal all wounds. (Jeremiah 30:17)

I decree that by Jesus' stripes, I am healed. (Isaiah 53:5)

I decree that sickness or death cannot have me or my family. We shall live a full life and declare the works of the Lord. (Psalm 118:17)

FINANCIAL BLESSINGS

I decree that I prosper in every area of my life, even as my soul prospers: spiritually, physically, mentally, emotionally and financially. (3 John 2)

I decree that God knows the plans for my life, a plan to prosper me, to give me hope and a bright future. (Jeremiah 29:11)

I decree that all the silver and gold belongs to God. Because it belongs to God, it is available for me to receive. (Haggai 2:8)

I decree the blessings of the Lord maketh me rich and He adds no sorrow to it. (Proverbs 10:22)

I decree the Lord is my Shepherd and I shall not want. (Psalm 23:1)

I decree that God gives us the power to get wealth, and I will receive this wealth to help sow into the kingdom of God. (Deuteronomy 8:18)

GOD'S PROTECTION

I decree that no weapon that is formed against me and my family will prosper. (Isaiah 54:17)

I decree that God has given His angels to keep charge over me and my family, to protect us, and no evil shall come near us or near our dwelling.

I decree that God is my refuge and strength in times of trouble. (Psalm 91)

I decree Psalm 91 over me, my family, friends, and divine connections.

I thank the Lord that we dwell in the secret place of the Most High and abide under the shadow of the Almighty. In the Name of Jesus. Amen.

THE ARMOR OF GOD
PUT ON THE WHOLE ARMOR OF GOD

Let's Put It On!

Don't let your momma, your daddy, your sister, your brother, your auntie, your uncle, your………….. cousin!

Don't let your husband, your wife, your children, your great great grandchildren, your nieces, your nephews, your siblings, your grandparents, your spiritual siblings, your spiritual parents.

Don't let no one leave the house without the armor of God on.

The armor of God helps you to fight against the plots and schemes of the enemy.

The armor helps you to stand against the enemy.

Make sure you are praying in the spirit. Make sure you are praying in the natural.

Make sure you pray for yourself and pray for God's people all around the world,

in Jesus name!

The Helmet of Salvation - WE PUT IT ON!

The Sword of the Spirit - WE PUT IT ON!

The Shield of Faith - WE PUT IT ON!

The Breastplate of Righteousness - WE PUT IT ON!

Our Feet Shod with the Preparation of the Gospel of Peace - WE PUT IT ON

And Our Belt Gird with Truth - WE PUT IT ON!

WE PUT IT ON! WE STAND WITH GOD!

WE PUT IT ON! WE STAND FOR GOD!

WE PUT IT ON!

WE PUT IT ON!

WE PUT IT ON!

IN JESUS NAME! IN JESUS NAME! IN JESUS NAME!

GLOOOORYYY HALLELUJAH!

THANK YOU, JESUS! THANK YOU, JESUS! THANK YOU, JESUS!

LORD, WE PRAISE YOU!

LORD, WE WORSHIP YOU!

LORD, WE HONOR YOU!

LORD, WE MAGNIFY YOUR NAME!

LORD, YOU ARE HOLY!

LORD, YOU ARE RIGHTEOUS!

MOST HIGH GOD, WE THANK YOU!

IN JESUS NAME!

(Ephesians 6 : 10 - 18)

THANKFUL

After reading the Bold Amazing Message From God Volume 1, what revelations are you thankful for?

_____
_____
_____
_____
_____
_____
_____
_____
_____
_____
_____
_____
_____
_____
_____
_____
_____
_____
_____
_____
_____
_____
_____

NOTES

NOTES

NOTES

NOTES

ABOUT THE AUTHOR

JJ Fox Hatch is a wife, mother, pastor, author, motivational speaker, media host, producer and business woman. JJ is the Pastor of WCM The Church, Founder of JJFH International, Mouthpiece for God, and deliverer of The BAM: The Bold Amazing Message From God. To learn more about JJ, go to JJFOXHATCH.COM.

Thank you to everyone who has taken the time to read this book.
I love you and there's nothing you can do about it.

JJ Fox Hatch

Made in the USA
Columbia, SC
29 September 2024

42662485R00162